MYTH INTO ART

How did the visual artist adapt mythological tales from Greek literature to the medium of painted pottery? *Myth into Art* is an introduction to this critical field of Greek iconography. The book focuses on the problem of narrative, the different means by which poet and painter tell the same story, rather than presenting a conventional survey of Greek myths. The approach is a comparative one, with excerpts from Greek authors set alongside the corresponding images within the text. The book is less a retelling of the myths than an interpretation of how they were rendered.

Thirty well known myths are treated, covering the principal texts from the Homeric epics to the tragedies of fifth-century Athens. The artistic material, featuring 129 black-and-white illustrations, concentrates on the black- and red-figure vases of Athens and South Italy from the sixth to the fourth century B.C. The book is thus an introduction both to the myths themselves and to the use of vase-painting as an essential primary source, alongside the texts, for an appreciation of the Greek view of myth.

Myth into Art shows how the Greek artist was influenced by the poetic sources on which he drew and how the artist communicates with the viewer in a fundamentally different way from the poet and his audience. It is directed primarily at undergraduate students of Classical civilization, mythology, Greek literature and art.

H. A. Shapiro is Professor of Classics at the University of Canterbury, Christchurch, New Zealand.

MYTH INTO ART

Poet and Painter in Classical Greece

H. A. Shapiro

London and New York

First published 1994
by Routledge
11 New Fetter Lane, London EC4P 4EE

Simultaneously published in the USA and Canada
by Routledge
29 West 35th Street, New York, NY 10001

Reprinted 1995

Typeset in 10/12pt Garamond by
Florencetype Ltd, Stoodleigh, Devon
Printed and bound in Great Britain by
Redwood Books, Trowbridge, Wiltshire

British Library Cataloguing in Publication Data
A catalogue record for this book is available from the British Library

Library of Congress Cataloguing in Publication Data
A catalogue record for this book is available from
the Library of Congress

ISBN 0-415-06793-6

For my mother
Rose W. Shapiro
to whom I owe the title of this book
and much else

CONTENTS

ILLUSTRATIONS

All photos are reproduced courtesy of the museum or collector unless otherwise specified. The following photos were kindly provided by the German Archaeological Institute: Figs. 18, 30, 31, 36, 37, 55, 62, 70, 71, 72, 88, 103, 112, 113, 126.
All dates are B.C.

PREFACE

The comparative study of mythology in Greek literature and art was pioneered by Carl Robert, in his book *Bild und Lied*, published in 1881; I have written this book partly in the belief that a new *Bild und Lied* would be useful to English-speaking students for whom Robert and other German scholarship are inaccessible. It is true that in recent years, French scholars have taught us new and interesting ways of looking at the images on Greek vases, applying principles of semiotics and structuralism, but the reader will not find any trace of that approach here. I doubt that Robert was any less sophisticated in his reading of Greek visual imagery than the modern iconographer and make no apologies for the unabashedly old-fashioned approach employed here.

I am, like all scholars of iconography, most of all indebted to two influential writers whose work is too seldom translated, Karl Schefold and Erika Simon. Schefold's recently completed series of five volumes on mythological imagery from the Archaic to the Hellenistic periods is far more comprehensive than this little book could hope to be and should be consulted at least for the many beautiful illustrations, if not for Schefold's extraordinarily sensitive appreciation of both Greek poetry and the art of the vase-painter. Similarly, Erika Simon has molded the present generation of iconographers with her many publications of the past forty years, and whatever interpretive skill I may possess is largely owed to the example of her work.

The other reason I have written this book is that I felt I had something to say about the narrative techniques of Archaic and Classical vase-painters that has not been said and illustrated systematically before. Although there have been many specialized studies on the problem of narrative published in recent years, all of them building on the work of Carl Robert, there has not been a general introduction to "reading" Greek narrative art. This aspect of the book is addressed both to students and to my fellow classicists, in particular philologists and literary critics who may not have found easy access to the visual sources that complement surviving texts.

This is not a handbook of Greek myths, for it deals with only some thirty out of the thousands that survive. I see these thirty rather as a collection of "test cases" for the comparative study of poetic and pictorial narrative. The criteria for selection are simple: I have chosen only those myths for which we have (*a*) a relatively full retelling in an extant literary work from Homer to Euripides and (*b*) a group of at least three or four preserved representations from the seventh to the fourth century. Only a few myths that meet these criteria have had to be omitted. Wherever possible, all the painted surfaces of a vase are illustrated, and the discussion focuses on how the finest painters combined several scenes into a narrative program.

The decision to organize the book according to the three principal literary genres, rather than into mythological or artistic categories, was inspired by a model proposed by Karl Schefold (*GHG* 272–79). He suggested that the imagery of the Archaic period can be divided into three successive modes that he calls "epic," "lyric," and "dramatic." Although not agreeing with Schefold's argument in detail, I have tried to adapt the model as an organizing principle. This will again perhaps make the book more accessible to classicists, but I hope it will not deter art-historians and others.

Although this book is the product of many years of looking at Greek vases and thinking about how they tell a story, the writing itself took place over a relatively brief period of time in the summer of 1992. This concentrated period of writing would not have been possible without both the financial support of the John Simon Guggenheim Memorial Foundation and the hospitality of three institutions with superb libraries: the American Academy in Rome; the Deutsches Archäologisches Institut, Berlin; and the American School of Classical Studies at Athens. I wish to thank all these institutions and especially Professor Helmut Kyrieleis, President of the DAI, for the invitation to Berlin and a generous stipend during my stay there.

Many friends and colleagues in museums throughout the world responded promptly and generously to my requests for photographs. Ingrid Rowland kindly checked my translations of Stesichoros. Finally, I wish to thank Richard Stoneman at Routledge, who suggested this project to me and was very supportive along the way.

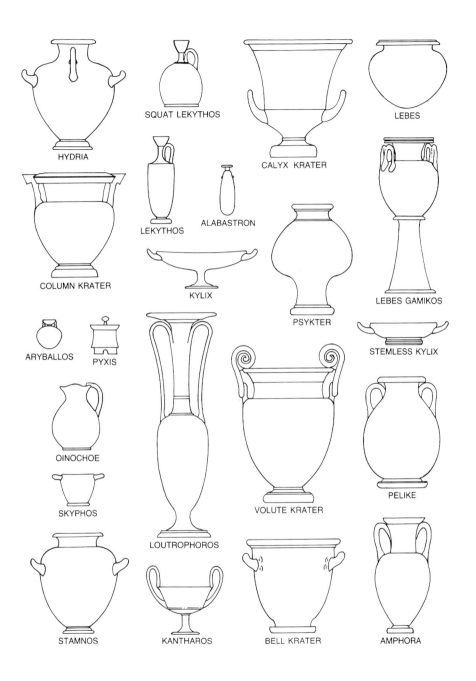

Names and shapes of Athenian vases

1

INTRODUCTION

THE WORLD OF GREEK MYTH

What we call mythology was, for the Greeks, the early history of their own people. They saw themselves in a direct line of descent from men of the Heroic Age, a period that modern archeological research would identify with the Late Bronze Age, ca. 1400–1200 B.C. Those heroes were, in turn, never more than two or three generations removed from that of the Olympian gods. Thus the gods, the heroes, and the "historical" Greeks of the Classical age formed, in their own view, one long continuum, albeit disturbed by periodic movements of peoples, invasions, colonization and the like. No wonder Hesiod, the Boeotian poet of the early seventh century, could complain that his own era, the Iron Age, was by far the worst in man's history. For once men and gods had mingled freely with one another and were part of one extended family; but in Hesiod's time, the gods seemed remote and uncaring, leaving man to eke out a miserable existence on his own.

In those hard times one of the Greeks' few remaining pleasures was the memory of that earlier time, the many tales of heroes and gods that had been passed down over the long centuries conventionally known as the "Dark Age." Only a generation or two before Hesiod, the poet we know as Homer had shaped some of these stories into a definitive form, as the *Iliad* and *Odyssey*. Even though these two epics cover only a fraction of the whole corpus of heroic saga, their most lasting impact was in creating a unified vision of the Heroic Age, of the nature of the gods and heroes, their relationship to one another, of fundamental issues of life and death.

At the divine level, Homer defined a pantheon presided over by Zeus, the "father of gods and men." It is itself an extended family, with most of its members either Zeus' siblings (sisters Demeter and Hera, also his wife; brothers Poseidon and Hades) or his various offspring (Athena, Apollo and Artemis, Ares, Hermes, Aphrodite). The intermarrying of gods and mortals is a practice well illustrated in Homer, through their offspring: Aeneas, son of Aphrodite by the Trojan noble Anchises; Sarpedon, the Lycian prince

1

and son of Zeus; Achilles, son of the sea goddess Thetis by the Thessalian hero Peleus; and many others. The offspring all belong to the race of heroes, who, in the last analysis, despite their "godlike" qualities, are defined by their mortality. Because it is the fact of death that separates the heroes from gods, which in the end makes them so much more interesting, many of the myths turn on the motif of the death of a hero. Even when a story celebrates the prowess of a hero in his prime, this is usually demonstrated at the cost of another's life.

Within the narrow focus of his two poems, Homer also managed to delineate one of the key aspects of Greek myth, its geographical dimension. The Greek army at Troy includes heroes from the whole length and breadth of the Greek mainland and the Aegean islands. The Trojan allies number several from Asia Minor with close ties to Greece through immigration and intermarriage. These are all summarized in the great Catalog of Ships in Book 2 of the *Iliad*. Greece is a small country in the modern world, but in antiquity the Greeks perceived an endless variety in the geography of their homeland and felt a powerful sense of identification with a native place. For them there were no "Greek" heroes, but Argive, Theban, Athenian, Corinthian, Cretan heroes, and so on, including the places in the Catalog of Ships that can no longer be located.

It would be left for other poets, who themselves originated in different parts of the Greek world, to gather the tales of heroes of their own city or region. Homer himself, whatever his origin (perhaps the island of Chios, as ancient tradition believed), is remarkably free of geographical attachments and seems to know the royal genealogies and myth history of every region of Greece. The *Odyssey*, of course, is about one hero from the island of Ithaca, but it is above all a poem of journey and discovery, and as such has a global perspective and a keen awareness of places outside the Greek world entirely (Egypt, Phoenicia). Every hero is localized in a particular place, yet each develops in the course of his career a network of contacts and relations, through common enterprises (the Trojan War, the voyage of the Argo) and travel abroad. It is in the interweaving of the many local traditions, the interconnections and interactions of one royal house with another, that the vast tapestry of Greek myth is created.

THE PLACE OF THE POET

This book is organized around the three principal genres of poetry in Archaic and Classical Greece. To some degree they form a chronological sequence, even if there were periods when more than one was practised. Modern opinion considers that epic poems in hexameter verse may have existed hundreds of years before Homer and circulated in oral form, performed by singers like Demodokos and Phemios in the *Odyssey*; but for us, epic poetry means primarily the two poems composed by Homer, probably in the second half of the eighth century. Ancient tradition preserves the names of several other epic poets, but none seems to have lived as early as Homer, and their poems, judged already in antiquity the work of inferior imitators of Homer, have not survived. This is a grievous loss, since, apart from the question of literary merit, these epics contained the whole corpus of heroic myths in their earliest organized telling: the Trojan War, both before and after the short excerpt of its tenth year recounted in the *Iliad*; the homecomings of the Greek heroes from Troy, other than Odysseus; the royal genealogies of Thebes and other major centers; the deeds and adventures of Herakles; and much more. Often visual sources are our best means of reconstructing the contents of these lost epics.

Hesiod is today also reckoned an epic poet, because he shared the dactylic hexameter of Homeric verse, although the subject and the structure of his poetry are quite unhomeric. There is, however, another reason why the ancients often referred to Hesiod and Homer in the same breath. Although written later, Hesiod's *Theogony* can be read as "background" to Homer's *Iliad*: that is, the *Iliad* describes a particular moment in the history of the cosmos, when Zeus and his family, from their home on Mt. Olympos, observe and control the destiny of mankind; from Hesiod we learn that this was not always so, but that Zeus is actually the youngest in a long line of divine rulers, his struggle to establish himself in power echoing that of many mortal kings. It was only with the combination of Homer and Hesiod that later Greeks could orient themselves with respect to the cosmos and their place in it.

The seventh and sixth centuries were the "Lyric Age of Greece," as A. R. Burn dubbed it, because poets in all parts of the Greek world experimented with new forms and new metres, but usually setting their songs to the music of the lyre. All these poets were conscious of standing in the shadow of Homer, and some sought to avoid the comparison by writing short, intensely personal or occasional poetry far removed from the epic tradition. Others, however, recognized the creative possibilities of recasting epic material in various ways – for example, by detaching a single heroic episode from its epic context and elaborating it into a self-contained poem. Perhaps the most successful of these poets was Stesichoros, from Sicilian Himera, for whom many substantial works on a wide range of heroes are attested and one, on Herakles and Geryon, partially preserved on papyrus.

Among the last poets of the Lyric Age were Pindar and Bacchylides, both commissioned to write occasional verse for athletic victors and religious festivals. For Pindar, Homer and the Epic Cycle were far enough in the past that he could distance himself and even question their authority when the received version conflicted with his own vision of gods and heroes. Thus began a dialog between the Classical Greeks and their own heroic past that kept the myths alive and insured their continuing relevance in everyday life.

From the second quarter of the fifth century, that dialog was carried on primarily through the medium of tragic drama. In Athens itself this meant productions in the Theatre of Dionysos that extended the performance of poetry from small private occasions or religious sanctuaries with a limited audience to civic events accessible to all the citizenry; not only that, but the visual dimension of actors in performance must have given the old tales an immediacy that no Archaic poet/singer could match.

The three tragedians whose work (or a fraction of it) survives, Aeschylus, Sophocles, and Euripides, each handled the conventions of drama in different ways. However, each in his own way used heroic myth as a vehicle for reflecting on the most pressing issues of his day: political, social, religious. Nor did they ever shy away from treating a subject that had already been dramatized by another playwright, for they recognized that each myth was open to multiple interpretations. Although we do not have the epics preserved from which they drew their material, we can infer that they seldom regarded these as fixed or sacrosanct; rather, the process of mythmaking was as alive and vigorous in the fifth century as in Homer's own time.

THE PLACE OF THE ARTIST

The early development of the figural arts in Greece followed a trajectory parallel to that of heroic saga. In the Late Bronze Age, as the tales of heroes were first being shaped, painters of large frescoes and clay vases were thriving in artistic centers from Mainland Greece to Crete and the Cyclades, even on Cyprus. Many of their ambitious compositions look like illustrations of pre-Homeric epic and have been interpreted as such in recent years (Fig. 1). But with the collapse of Mycenaean civilization in the twelfth century B.C., this art-form disappeared, and even on decorated pottery no human figure would appear for several hundred years. The rediscovery of a figural style, on monumental funeral vases in the middle of the eighth century, corresponds exactly with the period when Homer would have been starting to gather the old stories into the 'rediscovered' medium of epic verse.

The question whether any of the so-called Late Geometric vase-painters, working in the second half of the eighth century, set out to represent specific heroic myths is a hotly debated one. There can be no question that many of their compositions are 'narrative,' in that they tell a story; however, the means at the painter's disposal did not allow him to be as specific as the modern iconographer would like. Probably these scenes presented no problems of interpretation for the contemporary viewer. So, for example, the scene on a Late Geometric bowl (Fig. 2), of a man and woman embarking on a big oared ship, looks unquestionably like a heroic subject and not one drawn from everyday life. However, whether it represents Paris taking Helen on board to set sail for Troy, or Theseus leading Ariadne away from Crete, or yet another mythological couple, is, at least to our eyes, left open.

4

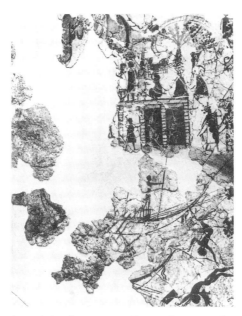

Figure 1 Shipwreck and landing party. Fresco fragment from Akrotiri, Thera. Athens, National Museum. Ca. 1450. After S. A. Immerwahr, *Aegean Painting in the Bronze Age* (University Park/London, 1989) pl. 27.

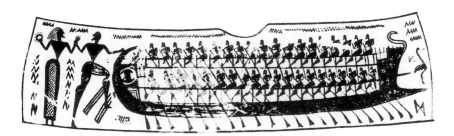

Figure 2 The abduction of Helen by Paris (?). Late Geometric bowl from Thebes. London, British Museum 1899.2–19.1. Ca. 750–700. After K. Schefold, *Frühgriechische Sagenbilder* (Munich, 1964) pl. 5c.

The question, then, is not when Greek artists first depicted heroic stories, but how they developed the narrative technique of making these stories immediately recognizable and increasingly complex, within the confines of the pot surface (since large-scale wall-painting seems not to have been re-invented until well into the sixth century). Here the seventh century, in spite of the impoverished state of our evidence, appears to have made all the most important advances. The first, perhaps, was simply the choice of subjects that, thanks to one or two basic narrative or iconographic elements, could be rendered with utter specificity. Thus, the simple combination of a human giant and a man or men driving a stake into his eye (see Figs. 30–32) could only be the blinding of Polyphemos. A second major advance of the Orientalizing style of the seventh century over the Geometric was the creation of a language of gesture and facial expression that greatly enriches the narrative. The figure of Klytaimestra as she witnesses the murder of her paramour Aegisthus (see Fig. 95) speaks volumes to those who know the story. Third, the seventh-century artist, capitalizing on the rapid spread of the alphabet throughout the Greek world, recognized its practical application in labeling his figures to make them readily identifiable. Where the subject is perfectly clear even without inscriptions, as in the suicide of Ajax (see Fig. 106), we can only think that the painter added them either to show off his own literacy or to appeal to a certain kind of clientele.

By the sixth century, we may assume that a great deal of epic poetry, by Homer and others, was circulating in oral form and, increasingly, in written form as well. We have evidence, for example, that 'authentic' texts of Homer were brought to or edited in Athens in the time of the Peisistratid tyrants (560–510). There were, in addition, the itinerant poets, like Stesichoros, performing their work at public events in the major religious and urban centers. Artists therefore had easy access to a wide range of material, and this is reflected in a veritable explosion of mythological representations from the early years of the sixth century. Although Corinthian vase-painters had rivaled Athenian in both quality and narrative sophistication (cf. Fig. 106), various market factors drove Corinthian wares into decline by the mid-sixth century, leaving Attic black-figure as our primary corpus of mythological scenes for the High Archaic period. These were also the years of the development of architectural sculpture as a medium of complex narrative. The continuous Ionic friezes of the Siphnian Treasury at Delphi, for example, are at times strikingly reminiscent of the Homeric vision of the Olympian gods.

The invention of the red-figure technique in Athens ca. 530–525 did not mark a sharp break in subject-matter, especially since black-figure continued in intensive production for another two generations. It is, nevertheless, astonishing how close a correlation exists in many cases between subject-matter and technique; that is, there are scenes that never made the transition to early red-figure (e.g. Herakles and Nessos, see Figs. 110–113) or were first introduced by the early generations of red-figure painters (e.g. Sarpedon, see Figs. 12 and 13).

There is barely a single mythological subject that can be said to enjoy continuous popularity in Attic vase-painting from early black-figure to late red-figure. The painters' repertoire was constantly in flux, partly in response to outside stimuli, such as new literary works (e.g. the Theseus cycle, see Figs. 76 and 77) or, later on, dramatic performances (cf. Fig. 102), but partly also reflecting the internal dynamics of an art-form. At a certain point, some subjects had simply run their course – for example, the many animal and monster combats of Herakles that lost their appeal by the end of the sixth century (e.g. Geryon, see Figs. 46–51). The imagery of Greek myth never constituted a religious dogma, in the way that Christian iconography did, and could thus be much freer in both its choice of subject and mode of representation. The average Greek did not need pictures of the gods and heroes, as medieval or Renaissance man needed images of Christ and the Virgin. The painted vases that are the main subject of this book were mainly used in a purely secular and domestic context, most of them at the symposium, or drinking-party. If the Greek chose to surround himself with these images, then it was more for esthetic than religious reasons.

The red-figure pottery industry, like the city of Athens as a whole, was dealt a tremendous blow by the long years of struggle and ultimate defeat in the Peloponnesian War. Politically, the city recovered remarkably fast, but the potters and painters did not, and in the first half of the fourth century their craft died a slow and (to our eyes) painful death; but as early as the 430s some Athenians had set up shop in the colonies of Southern Italy and planted the seeds of a thriving industry in red-figure vase production that would continue nearly to the end of the fourth century. Its major centers were in the areas of Taranto (Apulian), Metaponto (Lucanian), and Capua (Campanian). Although, after this first generation of immigrants, the great majority of South Italian painters probably never set foot in Greece, it is a testimony to the strength and endurance of Greek tradition, in colonies established in some cases over 300 years previously, that mythological representations now reach a new high point of originality and fidelity to literary sources. Often these scenes can be recognized as responses to productions of Attic tragedies that were, for these Greek cities in the west, one of the primary direct links with their cultural heritage.

In the Hellenistic Age – after Alexander the Great and beyond the scope of this book – Greek art entered a new relationship with its mythological past. In the wake of the scholarly study and editing of Homer as a "classic" text, a new type of pottery was created – the so-called "Homeric bowls" – placing vignettes from the epic alongside extracts from the text (Fig. 3). From here it was not a long step to the illustrated manuscripts of the Early Christian and Byzantine periods, completing a direct line of development in Greek narrative art from the time of Homer himself.

POET AND PAINTER: NARRATIVE STRATEGIES

That the visual arts have fundamentally different ways of telling a story from the poet or singer was apparent even to the first students of Greek art, in the eighteenth century. The great German writer Gotthold Ephraim Lessing, whose *Laokoon* of 1766 was the first serious study of Classical art, gave his book the subtitle "über die Grenzen der Malerei und Poesie" (On the

Boundaries between Painting and Poetry). Over a century later, the modern study of narrative in Greek art was put on a firm footing by another German scholar, Carl Robert, whose laconic title epitomizes the comparative approach that he inherited ultimately from Lessing: *Bild und Lied* (Image and Song). Robert and a younger contemporary in Vienna, Franz Wickhoff, sought to systematize Greek narrative by defining and coining names for several different methods. Their German terminology eventually made the transition to English, mainly through the work of the Byzantinist Kurt Weitzmann in 1947, but not without much disagreement, both conceptual and linguistic. In the past fifteen years, the scholarly discussion of narrative has once again been revived, with particular intensity but little consensus. The following sketch of four methods of narration in Greek and Roman art is adapted from the Cambridge archeologist Anthony Snodgrass, who has made especially thoughtful contributions to the ongoing discussion:

1 Monoscenic: a depiction of a single moment in a particular story which preserves the unity of time and space. In other words, if the story were happening in real life, the picture could be a photograph taken at one particular moment.
2 Synoptic: a combination of several different moments or episodes from a story into a single picture. There is, therefore, no unity of time and often none of place either. The picture corresponds to an impossible moment that no photograph could capture, but no figure occurs more than once.
3 Cyclic: a series of discrete episodes from a longer story that are physically separated from one another (e.g. metopes on a temple), and the figure of the protagonist is repeated in each episode.

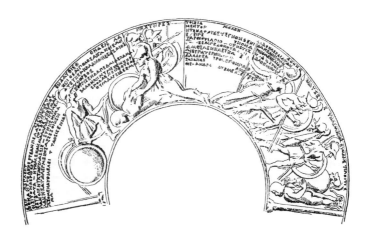

Figure 3 Scenes from Book 22 of the *Odyssey* (the slaying of the Suitors). Hellenistic bowl with relief decoration. Berlin, Pergamon Museum 3161. Ca. 150. After U. Sinn, *Die Homerischen Becher* (Berlin, 1979) 91.

8

4 Continuous: a variant of the cyclic, in which there are no physical boundaries between the individual episodes.

The last type, the continuous, is agreed to be an invention of both Ancient Near Eastern and Roman art, but was not known to the Greeks, and thus will not be encountered in this book.

The other three methods all occur in Archaic and Classical Greek art and their chief interest lies in considering when and under what circumstances artists preferred one or the other. To a modern viewer, the monoscenic is the most "basic," in that it corresponds to our perception of reality. No artist had to consciously *choose* the monoscenic method, and it occurs in all periods of Greek art. The synoptic, in contrast, seems to be a peculiarly Archaic Greek form of narration and as such has attracted the most interest and the most controversy. It occurs as early as a proto-Attic amphora of ca. 670 (see Figs. 30 and 31), where the Cyclops drinking the wine offered him by Odysseus and his blinding with the red-hot stake – two quite separate episodes in Homer's narrative – are combined in one picture. A century later, a Laconian cup combines not only these two moments, but a third, the Cyclops feasting on Odysseus' men (see Fig. 32).

Snodgrass has argued persuasively that the synoptic method was not so much an intellectual decision of the Greek artist as a way of conceptualizing that came naturally to him, particularly as he was not conditioned by photographic images to assume the unity of time and space. In what follows, I adopt the view, generally in agreement with this, that the Greek artist's first priority was often to cram as much of a story as he could into the confines of his picture, and if this meant what we would call a "violation" of the unity of time or place, he either was unaware of it or did not care. This applies equally to the Early Archaic vase-painter and to the fourth-century painters of Athens and South Italy, who in some instances were trying to squeeze a whole tragedy onto a single picture panel (see Figs. 118–120; 129).

The cyclic method is mostly associated with Classical and Hellenistic art, but it is now clear that its origins are Late Archaic, both on metopes such as those of the Athenian Treasury at Delphi and on red-figure cups showing the deeds of Theseus (see Figs. 76 and 77). In the case of the metopes, it is easy to see how the architectural form itself might have suggested such a thematically related cycle. The Theseus cups are harder to explain, since they occur suddenly, about 510, in the midst of a long-established vase-painting tradition that had never experimented with anything comparable. It may be that the missing link should be sought in large-scale wall-painting, which was in its infancy at this time and may have encouraged narrative innovations of which we are unaware. Certainly by the middle of the fifth century, vase-paintings reflect certain techniques of wall-painting that alter the shape of the narrative, such as the placing of figures on superimposed picture planes (see Fig. 64).

In this book, we shall not enter the debate on the terminology of Greek narrative or its theoretical foundations, but rather try to approach each image with an unprejudiced eye, asking how the artist went about the task of translating a story he had heard or read or seen on the stage into visual terms. It will emerge that pictorial artists do see the world differently from poets, who fashion their stories out of words. There is also a very different relationship between the artist and his "audience" (that is, the viewer) from that of the poet or performer and his listeners. (Since no Greek poetry was intended to be appreciated solely as a written text, we need not worry about the relationship between author and reader.)

The things that the artist considers it important to convey to the viewer may not correspond to those that pass from poet to audience. We can no longer reconstruct the experience of hearing a performance by Homer or Stesichoros, or seeing a play of Aeschylus as the fifth-century Athenian saw it. When we look at a Greek vase, however, we may be sure that we are seeing the very same object that the original purchaser and his friends saw. In that sense, the visual arts of the Greeks speak to us more immediately and directly than their poetry ever can. However, there is a danger in this as well, for we are seeing the objects with very different eyes and different cultural, esthetic, and perceptual assumptions. It is our job to try to think ourselves into the world of the Greek viewer and see his own myths in his own art as he would have seen it.

2

EPIC

HOMER'S *ILIAD*: THE TROJAN WAR

The *Iliad* opens in the tenth year of the Greek siege of Troy, brought on by the theft of Helen, wife of King Menelaos of Sparta, by the young Trojan prince Alexandros (Paris). The poet announces in the first verse that he will sing "the wrath of Achilles," and this motif does indeed provide the structure of the entire poem, until its final resolution in Book 24, when Achilles returns to Priam the body of his son Hektor. By this point, the source of Achilles' wrath had changed to something far more devastating in its effect on him, the death of his beloved friend, Patroklos, at the hands of Hektor.

Book 1: Briseis

Initially, the wrath of Achilles had been caused by the insult to his honor of having his slave-girl, Briseis, taken away from him by the Greek commander, Agamemnon. Through the early scenes of *Iliad* 1 the hostility between the two heroes builds to a crescendo of hatred and name-calling that goes far beyond the matter at hand and suggests that nine years of fruitless siege have strained relations between them to the breaking-point. Agamemnon has learned that he must return his own prize, Chryseis, to her father, a priest of Apollo who had prevailed upon the god to bring down a plague on the Greek camp; but Agamemnon, as the most powerful of the Greek chieftains, cannot be without a suitable prize. To Achilles' reasonable assurance that, there being no extra, unallocated booty (i.e. slave-girls) on hand, Agamemnon can expect a much richer reward once Troy is taken, the latter reacts testily, threatening to help himself to another hero's girl, "your own, or that of Aias, or that of Odysseus" (1.138). This in turn provokes Achilles to vent long-pent-up frustration, that Agamemnon always claims the lion's share of the spoils while he, Achilles, does most of the hard fighting. He threatens to leave Troy and go home, a challenge to Agamemnon's authority that only stiffens his resolve to have Briseis, "that you may learn well how much greater I am than you" (1.185–86). Only

11

Athena's intervention stays Achilles' hand from drawing his sword against Agamemnon. Thus, in this brief exchange full of psychological insight, two proud and immature heroes move quickly from rational discourse to murderous wrath. The actual taking of Briseis from Achilles' tent is in this way invested with enormous tension, since it will have far-reaching consequences, although the poet's description of it is rather matter-of-fact and unemotional:

> Thus these were busy about the army. But Agamemnon
> did not give up his anger and the first threat he made to Achilleus,
> but to Talthybios he gave his orders and Eurybates
> who were heralds and hard-working henchmen to him: "Go now
> to the shelter of Peleus' son Achilleus, to bring back
> Briseis of the fair cheeks leading her by the hand. And if he
> will not give her, I must come in person to take her
> with many men behind me, and it will be the worse for him."
> He spoke and sent them forth with this strong order upon them.
> They went against their will beside the beach of the barren
> salt sea, and came to the shelters and the ships of the Myrmidons.
> The man himself they found beside his shelter and his black ship
> sitting. And Achilleus took no joy at all when he saw them.
> These two terrified and in awe of the king stood waiting
> quietly, and did not speak a word at all nor question him.
> But he knew the whole matter in his own heart, and spoke first:
> "Welcome, heralds, messengers of Zeus and of mortals.
> Draw near. You are not to blame in my sight, but Agamemnon
> who sent the two of you here for the sake of the girl Briseis.
> Go then, illustrious Patroklos, and bring the girl forth
> and give her to these to be taken away. Yet let them be witnesses
> in the sight of the blessed gods, in the sight of mortal
> men, and of this cruel king, if ever hereafter
> there shall be need of me to beat back the shameful destruction
> from the rest. For surely in ruinous heart he makes sacrifice
> and has not wit enough to look behind and before him
> that the Achaians fighting beside their ships shall not perish."
> So he spoke, and Patroklos obeyed his beloved companion.
> He led forth from the hut Briseis of the fair cheeks and gave her
> to be taken away; and they walked back beside the ships of the
> Achaians,
> and the women all unwilling went with them still. But Achilleus
> weeping went and sat in sorrow apart from his companions
> beside the beach of the grey sea looking out on the infinite water.

Iliad 1.318–50

With characteristic bravado, Agamemnon again adds his threat to come and

Figure 4 Briseis led away from Achilles' tent. Attic red-figure cup attributed to the Briseis Painter (name vase), side A. London, British Museum E76. Ca. 480.

take Briseis by force should Achilles resist, even though Achilles had just sought to pre-empt such a confrontation by assuring him, "with my hands I will not fight for the girl's sake, neither with you nor any other man, since you take her away who gave her" (1.298–99). Achilles, as so often later in the poem, is a melancholy figure, polite and stoic rather than excitable and impetuous. The scene also introduces for the first time Patroklos, who is not only Achilles' "beloved companion" and comrade-in-arms, but also a subordinate helper in the domestic life of the tent. Thus he is dispatched to fetch Briseis and hand her over to Agamemnon's henchmen.

Two Attic red-figure vases of ca. 480 B.C. depict Briseis' removal from the Myrmidons' camp. The more detailed of the two balances the scene of Briseis led away from Achilles (Fig. 4) with one not described by Homer but nevertheless a logical sequel, her arrival at Agamemnon's camp (Fig. 5). Each scene is composed of a long frieze of six figures bounded by the handles of the drinking cup, allowing each to unfold spatially just as the story unfolds temporally from one side to the other. Briseis' departure on side A is remarkably faithful to the spirit of the Homeric account, if not to every particular. The two heralds, one leading and one following her, may be presumed to be Talthybios and Eurybates. Briseis' unwillingness to go is expressed in her stance, stock-still, responding not at all to the Greek's grip on her wrist. The pair conforms exactly to an iconographical schema popular in Greek art, the young groom leading away his bride by the wrist (*cheir epi karpo*). Painter and viewer, of course, were well aware that this is not a wedding scene, yet the "contamination" may in fact have served the painter's narrative purpose in other ways. It is even reinforced by Briseis' having

13

drawn her mantle up over her head like a veil, a standard bridal motif. We are reminded that Briseis was more to Achilles than prize or concubine; she was promised to him in marriage, as she will later recall in a lament addressed to the dead Patroklos (19.297–99).

Achilles appears to sit within his tent, rather than outside it, yet we imagine his eye following the receding figure of Briseis. Swathed in drapery from head to toe, he is depicted in mourning (the right hand pressed against his forehead is also a gesture of ritual mourning), and although he now sits rigid and unmoved, we can well imagine the tears that will follow as soon as Briseis is out of sight. Of the two unnamed companions who watch Achilles with sympathy, one could be Patroklos, although his role here is finished once Briseis has been handed over, so he is of no interest to the artist.

The scene on the other side (see Fig. 5) is pure invention, but one that for the painter needed no textual authority, only common sense. We know from Book 9, the embassy to Achilles, that Briseis has indeed been living in Agamemnon's camp, although untouched by him (9.274–76). What is most striking in the painted scene is the absence of the one figure who would have lent it a dramatic edge – Agamemnon himself. Why, then, bother to imagine this moment at all? In its very indirection there is a kind of Homeric quality about the scene. The difference between Agamemnon's palatial camp and Achilles' modest tent is underscored by the architectural elements, two substantial Doric columns with entablature. The master is deep within, in almost Oriental seclusion. The nondescript Achaean nobles who loiter before the entrance to Agamemnon's headquarters also allude to both his importance and his inaccessibility. The pair engaged in friendly gossip are

Figure 5 Briseis arriving at Agamemnon's camp. Side B of the cup shown in Fig. 4 (p. 13).

Figure 6 Two Greek heroes discussing Briseis. Interior of the cup shown in Fig. 4 (p. 13).

especially reminiscent of a famous *Iliad* scene, in which the Trojan elders observe and comment on the cause of so much suffering – Helen (3.146–60). So too here, we may imagine these two, who have just caught a glimpse of Briseis as she passed, remarking on the lovely girl at the center of such a bitter feud. The cup's interior (Fig. 6) gives us two more of the Achaeans, also in animated discussion of the momentous events dispassionately spread over the exterior friezes. This is thus one of the earliest instances among red-figure cups in which a single epic theme links all three images.

Figure 7 Agamemnon leads Briseis away from Achilles' tent. Attic red-figure skyphos, attributed to Makron, side A. Paris, Louvre G146. Ca. 480–470.

The second preserved version of Briseis' departure for Achilles' camp, although exactly contemporary, is radically different in conception (Fig. 7). Only the herald Talthybios, marked by the kerykeion as well as a naming inscription, corresponds to the Homeric account. Otherwise, the painter would seem to be working from an alternative *Iliad*, one in which Agamemnon makes good on his threat to come himself to "confiscate" Briseis. Once again Briseis is dressed like a bride, now even performing the characteristic bridal gesture of lifting her veil with one hand, and once again she is led away by a firm tug of the wrist. However, her escort, in military dress, is now clearly labeled as "Agamemnon." In another striking departure, his second companion is Diomedes, an important Greek hero at Troy, but one who nowhere figures in the Homeric version of the Briseis episode. His presence has been seen as a kind of proleptic reference to the story depicted on the other side of the vase, the embassy to Achilles, which we shall consider presently.

Does our vase lend support to the conjecture that there was an alternate version in the epic tradition, in which Agamemnon in fact acted upon his threat to come and fetch Briseis? Such an argument has actually been made on purely textual grounds, since immediately after Briseis' departure, Achilles tells his mother, Thetis, that Agamemnon has himself taken his prize away (1.356), words that will later be echoed by Thersites in his diatribe against Agamemnon (2.240) and again by Nestor in urging Agamemnon to make amends (9.107). "The possibility begins to present itself that what began as a mere threat is being established in the minds of some of the characters – and, at odd moments, of the poet himself? – as what actually happened" (Kirk 1985: 72); and, we might add, in the mind of the vase-painter Makron. The addition of Diomedes, however, shows that Makron was not striving for complete fidelity to the text in any event. Since Diomedes does not, strictly speaking, belong to the embassy scene either (he argued that the embassy had been a mistake, 9.697), his presence can only be a general allusion to the fact that, as one of the younger and most enthusiastic of the Achaean heroes, he shows consistent loyalty to Agamemnon and to the Greek cause.

What Makron's scene gains in dramatic power by putting Agamemnon into physical contact with Briseis, it loses in pathos through the omission of Achilles. He appears instead as the focal point of the reverse (Fig. 8), and it thus becomes clear that the painter's primary narrative intent was the juxtaposing of two episodes with a direct thematic link, even if separated by considerable time and one-third of the *Iliad*.

Book 9: the embassy to Achilles

With the loss of Briseis, Achilles retires from the battlefield, determined to remain aloof until Agamemnon and the other Achaeans acknowledge that

16

Figure 8 Embassy to Achilles. Side B of the skyphos shown in Fig. 7 (p. 15).

they cannot win the war without him. To that end his mother extracts from Zeus a promise to favor the Trojan side for a while. Through the first third of the *Iliad*, the battle see-saws back and forth. Several single combats that promise a quick resolution (Menelaos vs. Paris in Book 3, Hektor vs. Ajax in Book 7) end inconclusively, owing to the intervention of various Olympian gods. Agamemnon comes to the bitter realization that he cannot hope to prevail now that Zeus has turned against him. In despair he is ready to abandon the siege and go home, an unworthy thought quickly banished by the cheerful determination of Diomedes. Instead, at the urging of Nestor, the wise old counsellor, Agamemnon will send an embassy to Achilles, offering him rich gifts (along with the return of Briseis, of course) if he will agree to rejoin the battle. For this delicate mission Nestor proposes a team of three: as leader, Phoinix, who is like a second father to Achilles, having reared him in the palace of King Peleus in Thessaly; Odysseus, most renowned of the Greeks for his cleverness and powers of persuasive speech; and Ajax, whose devotion to the Greek cause and utter lack of guile will underscore the sincerity of Agamemnon's offer. The scene of their reception by Achilles is remarkable for its portrayal of the hero's restraint and grace under pressure:

> Now they came beside the shelters and ships of the Myrmidons
> and they found Achilleus delighting his heart in a lyre, clear-sounding,
> splendid and carefully wrought, with a bridge of silver upon it,
> which he won out of the spoils when he ruined Eëtion's city.
> With this he was pleasuring his heart, and singing of men's fame,
> as Patroklos was sitting over against him, alone, in silence,
> watching Aiakides and the time he would leave off singing.
> Now these two came forward, as brilliant Odysseus led them,

and stood in his presence. Achilleus rose to his feet in amazement
holding the lyre as it was, leaving the place where he was sitting.
In the same way Patroklos, when he saw the men come, stood up.
And in greeting Achilleus the swift of foot spoke to them:
"Welcome. You are my friends who have come, and greatly I need
     you,
who even to this my anger are dearest of all the Achaians."

Then when he had roasted all, and spread the food on the platters,
Patroklos took the bread and set it out on a table
in fair baskets, while Achilleus served the meats. Thereafter
he himself sat over against the godlike Odysseus
against the further wall, and told his companion, Patroklos,
to sacrifice to the gods; and he threw the firstlings in the fire.
They put their hands to the good things that lay ready before them.
But when they had put aside their desire for eating and drinking,
Aias nodded to Phoinix, and brilliant Odysseus saw it,
and filled a cup with wine, and lifted it to Achilleus.

Iliad 9.185–98; 215–24

Achilles is the model host, Patroklos again the attentive, unobtrusive helper.
Although Achilles surely knows the meaning of this delegation and is
resolved to be unmoved by it, his treatment of his guests and patience in
hearing them out are no less cordial for that.

Figure 9 Embassy to Achilles. Attic calyx-krater, attributed to the Eucharides
Painter, side A. Paris, Louvre G163. Ca. 490.

A series of about a dozen Attic vases of the fifth century depicts the emissaries in Achilles' tent (Figs. 8 and 9). The cast of characters varies, as we shall see, but one element is nearly constant: the portrayal of Achilles as if in deep mourning, wrapped in a voluminous garment that sometimes covers his head and bent over like someone in physical pain. The moment within the narrative that is shown can be localized fairly closely, since Achilles always sits opposite Odysseus, the first of the three to address him. There is no sign of the food and drink that have just been consumed. Odysseus' characteristic pose has both hands clasped around the left knee, which is either lifted or slung over the right. The pose is often interpreted elsewhere in Greek art as one expressing impatience, but it is not clear that this would suit the context here, in which all three are at pains to conceal the exasperation they may feel at Achilles' intransigence. Rather, the gesture seems one of studied nonchalance, an attempt to put Achilles at ease and make him more receptive to Agamemnon's offer. Achilles, however, will not even meet Odysseus' gaze, and this image of utter dejection and refusal to communicate makes crystal-clear the ultimate failure of the mission.

The consistency with which this "mourning" Achilles appears on a half-dozen vases, on the one hand, and the stark contrast with the Achilles of *Iliad* 9, on the other – he is not only a lavish host, but voluble in the exchanges with his comrades – arouse suspicion that another telling of the story has intervened between Homer and the fifth-century vase-painters. Indeed, early in his career (ca. 490), the playwright Aeschylus presented a trilogy on the subject of Achilles at Troy whose first play, the *Myrmidons*, dealt with the embassy. Only a few scraps of the play survive, but the striking image of Achilles, muffled in his cloak and sitting in stony silence, made such an impression that Aristophanes could recall and make fun of it nearly a century later (*Frogs* 911–13).

What is less clear is whether any other departures from the Homeric version – the occasional substitution of Diomedes for Ajax, for example – can be attributed to Aeschylus' influence. In fact, apart from the central group of Achilles and Odysseus opposite one another, each painted version varies the other elements, both of setting and character. The earliest of the series decorates one side of an impressively large calyx-krater of about 490 (see Fig. 9) – that is, very close in date to Aeschylus' play. Achilles' now idle weapons hang on the imaginary wall of his tent, and a leopard-skin – the one touch of luxury in this otherwise spartan setting – upholsters his simple stool. Behind Odysseus stands Phoinix, not white-haired as he will be on some later vases, but still clearly the oldest of the company with his heavy drapery, tentative stance, and long walking-stick. The younger man casually posed behind Achilles, whom we would assume to be Ajax, is instead labeled "Diomedes." This is less likely due to Aeschylus than to a painter's rethinking of Homer, as when Makron sends Agamemnon to fetch Briseis (see Fig. 7). Diomedes plays a key role in *Iliad* 9, both at the beginning, persuading

Figure 10 Hypnos and Thanatos carry the dead Sarpedon from the battlefield. Side B of the calyx-krater shown in Fig. 9 (p. 18).

Agamemnon not to lose heart, and later, trying to dismiss the failed mission to Achilles and turn his comrades' thoughts back to the battle. Might the painter not have thought Diomedes would have been a better choice than Ajax to send on the embassy, Diomedes with his infectious good cheer and youthful enthusiasm for war?

Like Makron (see Figs. 7 and 8), the Eucharides Painter did not see the embassy to Achilles as an isolated episode, but rather as linked to another, now looking ahead to the chain of events, starting with the death of Sarpedon (see Fig. 10), that will finally end Achilles' boycott of the war. We shall consider this link in more detail in the next section. For Makron, the narrative connection between Briseis and the embassy is perhaps a more obvious one, but no less innovative for its time. His Achilles is not veiled like the Aeschylean character (see Fig. 8), and in other respects the scene comes closest to Homer's account of any we have. Ajax and Phoinix look on with keen interest while Odysseus makes their case.

At the end of the fifth century, a Greek painter working in Taras (modern Taranto) in South Italy decorated a large krater with the embassy to Achilles (Fig. 11). Apulian kraters often have many figures disposed on several levels, and the fragments that survive may represent only a small part of the scene. Nevertheless, the subject is unmistakable, and the principal characters are here: Achilles seated in his "tent" (actually a naiskos, or mini-temple, of the type usually representing the tomb on South Italian vases), holding his lyre (only part of the frame preserved); Patroklos seated just outside; and the arriving delegation of three. Although Apulian vases are often suspected to reflect revivals of Attic tragedy in the provinces, this scene looks much closer to the *Iliad* than to the *Myrmidons* of Aeschylus.

With the embassy to Achilles we encounter our first instance of this dual tradition in Classical iconography: epic subject-matter filtered through the lens of Classical drama, and then reinterpreted by artists who had access to both sources. Unfortunately, there is not a single case where we have preserved *both* literary versions along with the pictorial. Typically, the Attic tragedies that we do have preserved draw their material from parts of the Epic Cycle now lost, while for the embassy the situation is reversed – an Iliadic episode adapted into a play no longer extant.

Book 16: the death of Sarpedon

Returning to the battle still without their greatest fighter, the Greeks continue to lose ground through the middle books of the poem (10–15) and are eventually driven back to their own ships. Zeus' implacable opposition is nevertheless partly offset by the intervention of Hera, Athena, and Poseidon, all fervently pro-Greek. Finally, with the Trojans threatening to set fire to the whole Greek fleet, Patroklos can no longer sit idly by out of loyalty to Achilles. Wearing Achilles' own armor (to fool the Trojans into thinking Achilles himself has returned), he re-enters the fray and covers himself with the glory of many slain Trojans. His most successful, and

Figure 11 Embassy to Achilles. Apulian red-figure bell-krater fragment, attributed to the Sarpedon Painter. Heidelberg University, Arch. Inst. 26.87. Ca. 390–370.

fateful, encounter is against Sarpedon, leader of the Lycians, an Asiatic people fighting as allies of the Trojans. This hero had not only distinguished himself earlier as one of the strongest fighters, but had the distinction of being a son of Zeus, by a mortal woman. Seeing the death of his beloved son fast approaching, Zeus is deeply pained and briefly toys with the idea of trying to interfere in the course of fate to rescue him, until Hera reminds him what chaos and ill-feeling among the gods would follow from this.

Where a Homeric hero is cut down, there often ensues a fierce struggle for his body, his own comrades trying to rescue the corpse to give it proper burial, while the enemy hope to strip off the armor as booty and vent their fury by mutilating the corpse. Although Zeus has shown restraint up to this point, he cannot endure to see the body of Sarpedon so abused, and so he conceives a plan:

> But the Achaians took from Sarpedon's shoulders the armour
> glaring and brazen, and this the warlike son of Menoitios
> gave to his companions to carry back to the hollow ships.
> And now Zeus who gathers the clouds spoke a word to Apollo:
> "Go if you will, beloved Phoibos, and rescue Sarpedon
> from under the weapons, wash the dark suffusion of blood from him,
> then carry him far away and wash him in a running river,
> anoint him in ambrosia, put ambrosial clothing upon him;
> then give him into the charge of swift messengers to carry him,
> of Sleep and Death, who are twin brothers, and these two shall lay him
> down presently within the rich countryside of broad Lykia
> where his brothers and countrymen shall give him due burial
> with tomb and gravestone. Such is the privilege of those who have
>   perished."
> He spoke so, and Apollo, not disregarding his father,
> went down along the mountains of Ida, into the grim fight,
> and lifting brilliant Sarpedon out from under the weapons
> carried him far away, and washed him in a running river,
> and anointed him in ambrosia, put ambrosial clothing upon him,
> then gave him into the charge of swift messengers to carry him,
> of Sleep and Death, who are twin brothers, and these two presently
> laid him down within the rich countryside of broad Lykia.
>
> *Iliad* 16.663–83

The armor is expendable, but the body must not be harmed. It is Apollo whom Zeus chooses to oversee the operation of rescuing Sarpedon's body, not only because he is well disposed to the Trojan side, but because he was to the Greeks the healing god, as expressed in his cult title "Paian." Only moments earlier, Apollo had healed the wounded arm of Sarpedon's fellow Lycian, Glaukos, so that he could help fight for the body (16.510–31). Apollo in turn entrusts the body to the twins Hypnos (Sleep) and Thanatos

Figure 12 Hypnos and Thanatos carry the body of Sarpedon from the battlefield. Attic red-figure cup signed by Euphronios. Private collection. Ca. 520. After *Wealth of the Ancient World* (exhibition catalog, Fort Worth, 1983) 55.

(Death). This is the only place in the *Iliad* where these brothers take part in the action, although not long before, Hera had enlisted the help of Hypnos to keep Zeus asleep while she intrigued on behalf of the Greeks (14.231–41). Homer never tells us, however, just how he pictures these two creatures; that would be left to the vase-painters.

In the decade 520–510, Euphronios, the greatest master of the early red-figure style, introduced Sarpedon to the repertoire of Greek art (Figs. 12 and

Figure 13 Hypnos and Thanatos lift the body of Sarpedon. Attic red-figure calyx-krater signed by Euphronios. New York, Metropolitan Museum 1971.11.1. Ca. 515–510.

23

13). Indeed, the subject appealed to him so much that he depicted it twice, each time approaching the problem of narrative and composition quite differently. His earlier effort is modest in scale, decorating one side of a drinking cup (see Fig. 12), but already displays some of the monumentality of conception with which the name Euphronios would later become synonymous. Hypnos and Thanatos have hoisted the body from the ground and fairly stagger under the weight of it. They trudge off to the right, led by a comrade named Akamas. There is no sense of the supernatural so prominent in Homer, of the notion that Sarpedon's body will be tidied up and whisked off to Lycia as if by magic. Euphronios' vision here belongs strictly to the war-is-hell school. Apollo has obviously not washed, anointed, and clothed the body; rather, it has just been lifted from the dust of the battlefield, blood still gushing from the wounds. The Greeks have indeed stripped it of its armor, all but the bronze greaves (shin-guards). Sarpedon's proportions are massive – if the body were set upright, it would be a head taller than the other three. Could Euphronios have had in mind Homer's striking simile, that the wounded Sarpedon "fell, as when an oak goes down or a white poplar, or like a towering pine" (16.482–83)?

Stretched out like this, he looks almost emaciated, every rib and sinew showing. If artists of the Italian Renaissance had known Attic vases, this might have been their model for the *pietà*. The long flowing hair could be a reference to Sarpedon's eastern origins, or perhaps reflects the tumult from which the body has just been rescued. The ethos could not be more different from Homer's poignant but oddly sanitized version.

Just a few years later, Euphronios was ready to spread the Sarpedon story out on the broad canvas of that majestic, recently invented vessel, the calyx-krater (see Fig. 13). Everything is changed, but above all the spirit is much closer to the Homeric model. The moment depicted is a split-second earlier, as Hypnos and Thanatos begin to lift the body. Although Sarpedon is again larger than life, we do not see the strain of lifting such a great dead weight. Rather, what is emphasized is the gentleness and care with which the delicate operation is performed. Our faith in the supernatural powers of Hypnos and Thanatos is now considerably enhanced by their large, splendid wings, even if in other respects they remain identical in dress and appearance to the human warriors. Clearly the younger Euphronios had not pondered the question, if Sleep and Death can barely get Sarpedon's body off the battle-field, how would they get it all the way to Lycia? Even if Homer never mentions that these two are winged, this is surely a logical inference.

Overseeing the whole operation is Hermes, who does not figure at all in the Homeric account. However, he is the messenger of Zeus, as well as the conductor of the souls of the dead (*psychopompos*), and his presence is a perfect way of conveying the idea that all this is being done at Zeus' behest. Apollo, whom some might have expected to see here instead, would only have confused matters, since in the pictorial tradition that whole intermediary stage – the washing and dressing of the body – has been omitted. Lastly, two warriors, Leodamas and Hippolytos, flank the scene, but stand so stiff and unmoved that they seem to function more as signposts for the battlefield at Troy than as participants in the action.

In one final respect Euphronios has come much closer to the Homeric ethos in this version than in his earlier effort. By removing Sarpedon's beard and giving him the first down of an ephebe, he greatly heightens the pathos of his death. There is no reason to think Sarpedon was actually meant to be so young. Indeed, for Homer he is a commander of all the Trojan allies (12.290–325), and the mythological tradition gave him a wife and child back in Lycia; but for an Athenian audience of the Late Archaic age, it is precisely this beardlessness, along with the fine, flowing hair, that gives the figure the nobility and heroic beauty Homer means us to imagine. In artistic terms, Sarpedon echoes the kouroi, marble statues of aristocratic long-haired youths that marked the tombs of those who fell in battle or otherwise died in their youthful prime.

Despite Euphronios' great stature among the pioneers of red-figure, the death of Sarpedon never attained much popularity with later artists. The figures of the winged Sleep and Death, however, would enjoy a second career on Classical Athenian funerary vases, as bearers of the bodies of unnamed Athenians, both female and male. One of the few large-scale depictions of Sarpedon, a generation after Euphronios, also decorates a calyx-krater (see Fig. 10), although only the bare outlines of Euphronios' composition remain intact. Indeed, until the inscription naming Sarpedon was rediscovered in a recent cleaning, it was often doubted that the body was his. Now, of course, it seems obvious that it *had* to be Sarpedon, because of the subtle thematic connection with the embassy to Achilles on the obverse (see Fig. 9). Achilles' refusal to fight will only end with the death of his friend Patroklos, when the desire for vengeance overrides the proud disdain for Agamemnon; and Patroklos' fate is sealed once he has slain the beloved son of Zeus, Sarpedon, and, drunk with his own success, goes on to slaughter more Trojans against the advice of Achilles and the will of Zeus.

Apart from his "stripped-down" approach to narrative, removing all the incidental figures to focus on the essence of the story, the most radical departure of the Eucharides Painter is the re-imagining of Hypnos and Thanatos. The transformation from human warriors to Homeric *daimones* is now complete. In this light, the creatures of Euphronios' second version (see Fig. 13) – husky, mature hoplites with delicate wings grafted on – look like incongruous hybrids. These youthful sprites we can better imagine easily lifting the heavy corpse and flying it to Lycia. The one element the painter has learned well from Euphronios is the gentleness with which they lift the body, one cradling the head in his arms like a mother with her dead son.

Homer does not pursue the story of Sarpedon back to the hero's home-land of Lycia, but his insistence on the return of the body made this a natural

25

Figure 14 The body of Sarpedon brought to Lycia. Apulian red-figure bell-krater, attributed to the Sarpedon Painter, side A. New York, Metropolitan Museum 16.140. Ca. 390–370.

subject for the imagination of tragic playwrights. Aeschylus, whose interest in both non-Greek peoples and tragic mothers is well known from one of his extant plays, the *Persians*, took up the challenge in a now lost play called *Carians* or *Europa*. In typically Aeschylean fashion, he took considerable liberties with the Homeric source, first changing Sarpedon's parentage (in Homer his mother is Laodameia, *Iliad* 6.198) and ethnicity (from Lycian to Carian); but in more important respects he was faithful to the spirit of Homer, to judge from the fine illustration of the play by an Apulian vase-painter of the early fourth century (Figs. 14 and 15). The arrival of the body is greeted with surprise, which will soon, no doubt, turn to horror, by Europa and several other Lycian (or Carian) family members and attendants. The trappings of stage production are evident in both sets and costumes. The brothers Hypnos and Thanatos have undergone yet another metamorphosis. Hypnos' head is unfortunately missing, but assuming that he is also the winged creature who reappears on the reverse of the vase, talking to Hera, we may infer that he was shown youthful and beardless. Thus the "twins" of Homer and Archaic art are no longer identical, but fraternal, and there is ample precedent for this on Classical white lekythoi, which had sought to differentiate Hypnos from Thanatos in a variety of ways.

The reverse of the vase has been ingeniously interpreted as another scene from the same play, Europa and Sarpedon's mourning young wife, Pasithea, in the presence of Zeus and Hera. It is, as we shall see, not unusual for

26

Figure 15 Pasithea and Europa (wife and mother of Sarpedon) before Zeus and Hera. Side B of the bell-krater shown in Fig. 14 (p. 26).

Apulian artists to combine several scenes from a tragedy into one multi-level tableau (see e.g. Fig. 129). Much less common is the juxtaposing of two scenes on opposite sides of a vase, as here. In this respect, this early Apulian painter is closer to his Athenian ancestors than to the later, more characteristic Apulian style of the mid-fourth century.

Book 22: the dragging of Hektor's body

The last third of the *Iliad* returns to the hero who has been largely absent until now, although the poem will reach its conclusion before Achilles reaches the end of his own brief life. That story would be left for another poet to tell. After killing Sarpedon, Patroklos plunges headlong into a fatal confrontation with Hektor. This is, of course, in part necessary to set the stage for the showdown that every listener has been anticipating from the start: Achilles vs. Hektor, the best of the Achaeans against the best of the Trojans. For this, however, Achilles must have a new set of armor (his own having been stripped from Patroklos' body by the Trojans), courtesy of his mother and the god of the forge, Hephaistos.

Achilles re-enters the fray with the ferocity of a wild animal, slaughtering all in his way, until he finally catches up with Hektor in Book 22. The duel is a bit of an anti-climax in many ways. Hektor, cornered outside the walls of Troy, suffers a sudden and uncharacteristic loss of nerve and tries to run from Achilles' onslaught. Achilles, for his part, is less than heroic in victory, for Athena has orchestrated the whole encounter. She first deceives Hektor into standing his ground and fighting by pretending to be his brother and comrade Deiphobos, then, in the actual duel, secretly returns to Achilles the spear that had missed its mark. What gives the episode a measure of suspense is rather the question what will happen to Hektor after he is dead.

Knowing Achilles' brutal nature and fearing the worst from the start, Hektor offers a deal before the first exchange of spear casts: whichever of the two prevails will return the other's corpse for proper burial (22.254–59). Achilles is having none of it, so great is his lust for vengeance. Indeed, the actual killing of Hektor can hardly begin to satisfy Achilles' mad fury; he has in store much worse humiliation:

> In both of his feet at the back he made holes by the tendons
> in the space between ankle and heel, and drew thongs of ox-hide
>   through them,
> and fastened them to the chariot so as to let the head drag,
> and mounted the chariot, and lifted the glorious armour inside it,
> then whipped the horses to a run, and they winged their way
>   unreluctant.
> A cloud of dust rose where Hektor was dragged, his dark hair was
>   falling
> about him, and all that head that was once so handsome was tumbled
> in the dust; since by this time Zeus had given him over
> to his enemies, to be defiled in the land of his fathers.
>
> So all his head was dragged in the dust; and now his mother
> tore out her hair, and threw the shining veil far from her
> and raised a great wail as she looked upon her son; and his father
> beloved groaned pitifully, and all his people about him
> were taken with wailing and lamentation all through the city.
> It was most like what would have happened, if all lowering
> Ilion had been burning top to bottom in fire.
> His people could scarcely keep the old man in his impatience
> from storming out of the Dardanian gates; he implored them
> all, and wallowed in the muck before them calling on each man
> and naming him by his name.

Iliad 22.396–415

Not just Hektor's parents, but all Troy is plunged into pitiful mourning. Achilles' thoughts turn to the task of burying Patroklos, although his mistreatment of Hektor's corpse does not cease, since he drives his chariot, Hektor still attached, three times around Patroklos' bier, then leaves the body face-down in the dust, a grisly offering to his dead friend (23.13–25).

Once the funeral and its attendant games are complete, Achilles, still tormented with grief, returns to abusing poor Hektor:

> Then, when he had yoked running horses under the chariot
> he would fasten Hektor behind the chariot, so as to drag him,
> and draw him three times around the tomb of Menoitios' fallen
> son, then rest again in his shelter, and throw down the dead man
> and leave him to lie sprawled on his face in the dust. But Apollo
> had pity on him, though he was only a dead man, and guarded
> the body from all ugliness, and hid all of it under the golden
> aegis, so that it might not be torn when Achilleus dragged it.
>
> *Iliad* 24.14–21

Only now does his behavior become offensive to the gods, and Zeus must put a stop to it.

Black-figure Athenian vase-painters of the late sixth century, who loved Homeric stories and loved violence even more, briefly turned the dragging of Hektor's body into one of their favorite subjects. There is a surprising degree of consistency within this compact group of representations, although one stands out as unusually ambitious, complex, and powerful.

The artist of a hydria in Boston (Fig. 16) managed to distill in his crowded yet clearly articulated composition many moments spanning several books of the *Iliad*, to great dramatic effect. Achilles does not drive his own chariot, as in Homer, but is about to leap onto a moving car driven by an anonymous companion (when the *Iliad* names Achilles' charioteer, he is Automedon). This minor departure from the text allows the painter to give us one of the few renderings that capture all the skill and ferocity of the Homeric Achilles. It is an almost superhuman feat of skill and balance that he accomplishes, appropriate to "swift-footed Achilles," and it is surely no accident that this curious pose places him exactly astride the limp body of the dead Hektor. As Achilles looks back, he is face to face with Hektor's parents, Hecuba and Priam, as they stand within the porch of the palace, watching this gruesome spectacle. Hecuba's gesture, hand to head, is one of ritual mourning, while Priam's outstretched hand is a vain gesture of supplication to Achilles. The big Corinthian helmet, hiding all but Achilles' glaring eye, takes on in this context a rather sinister aspect. The notion that Hektor's parents had to witness the abuse of their son's body is, of course, already present in Homer, but it was the vase-painter's inspiration to bring them into such chillingly close proximity.

Achilles' horses disappear off the screen, as it were, as they round a large, white conical mound designated as the tomb of Patroklos. This is a reference to the third dragging of Hektor's body, after the burial of Patroklos in the Greek camp. Both space and time have been drastically compressed. The tiny armed and winged creature emerging from the mound is the eidolon, or spirit, of Patroklos, which seems to want to charge back into the fray. It is

Figure 16 Achilles dragging Hektor's body around the tomb of Patroklos. Attic black-figure hydria of the Leagros Group. Boston, Museum of Fine Arts 63.473. Ca. 510.

not unusual for Greek artists to depict a warrior's eidolon rising from or hovering beside his tomb; but here we cannot help but think of the scene when the ghost of Patroklos appears to the sleeping Achilles, impatient to be burned and buried so he can enter the Underworld (23.65–71). A snake rearing up from the tomb also alludes to the earth that covers over a hero when he goes down to the house of Hades.

Finally, there is the winged woman who in fact catches our eye first, since she is in the front plane, dashing in from stage-right. She must be Iris, the gods' messenger, but why her sudden appearance? For this we must return to the text, to Book 24. This is surely the painter's most daring leap of imagination in an already far-reaching vision. Once Zeus has decided how this sorry situation is to be resolved, the divine chain of command is set in motion. Iris is dispatched to deliver Zeus' command to Thetis, that she persuade her son to stop the outrage. This accomplished, Iris is sent out a second time, to tell Priam he must venture forth to Achilles' tent in order to ransom Hektor's body. This rather cumbersome communications network clearly did not suit the highly economical narrative of the painter, so instead he simply appropriates the figure of Iris to convey his own message. Since he has conveniently assembled all the protagonists, Iris' excited hand-gesture signals both the end of the dragging and the invitation to Priam to visit Achilles.

The vase is a prime example of the creative possibilities of visual narrative in the hands of a thoughtful and skillful artist. We can do no better than to quote Emily Vermeule, in her masterful publication of the vase:

> The painter has thus condensed a series of literary memories into a single impossible moment, blending incompatible motifs and episodes in a way that underscores all the emotional tensions at the end of the *Iliad* . . . he has brought all the critical acts of the drama into a single imaginative correlation which transcends the spatial and temporal limitations of narrative art in poetry.
>
> (Vermeule 1965: 42; 46)

Most other versions of the dragging of Hektor share this merging of episodes, although no other includes Priam and Hecuba, who give the Boston vase its extraordinary emotional power. Typical is the scene on the shoulder of a hydria in Munich (Fig. 17). In this long narrow frieze, there is

Figure 17 Achilles dragging the body of Hektor. Attic black-figure hydria of the Leagros Group, shoulder. Munich, Antikensammlungen 1719. Ca. 510–500.

31

less need for figures to overlap, and the pace of the action has considerably slowed. The horses have paused at the mound from which Patroklos' ghost emerges, allowing Achilles to dismount and savor the image of the dead Hektor momentarily gracing the tomb of the man whose life he took. Iris does not burst in on this quiet scene, but enters rather gingerly from the left, lifting her garment delicately with one hand and holding her herald's wand in the other. Achilles is not yet aware of her presence. In its contemplative quality the scene is a striking contrast to the frenzied action and high drama of the contemporary hydria in Boston.

Book 23: the funeral games for Patroklos

Achilles' abuse of Hektor's corpse could only be interrupted by the one task of much more pressing urgency, the burial of Patroklos. Homer's detailed description of the funerary ritual, stretching over several days, is a kind of textbook for much of our knowledge of Greek burial customs. Its final stage, as we have already seen, was the piling-up of an earthen mound to mark the tomb (see Figs. 16 and 17). No sooner was this accomplished than Achilles announced a series of funeral games in Patroklos' honor. The list of events sounds almost like the program of the ancient Olympics: boxing, wrestling, a foot-race, a mock duel, shot-put, archery, and javelin-throwing; but the real centerpiece of the contests, as it was also the most prestigious event at Olympia, was the chariot race. As with each subsequent competition, Achilles begins by setting out the prizes offered:

> First of all
> he set forth the glorious prizes for speed of foot for the horsemen:
> a woman faultless in the work of her hands to lead away
> and a tripod with ears and holding twenty-two measures
> for the first prize; and for the second he set forth a six-year-old
> unbroken mare who carried a mule foal within her.
> Then for the third prize he set forth a splendid unfired
> cauldron, which held four measures, with its natural gloss still upon it.
> For the fourth place he set out two talents' weight of gold, and for
> the fifth place set forth an unfired jar with two handles.
> *Iliad* 23.261–70

Five warriors enter themselves, with their teams of horses, in the contest. The next, and crucial, step is to determine the positioning of the five teams at the starting-gate, which is done by lot:

> They climbed to the chariots and deposited the lots. Achilleus
> shook them, and the first to fall out was that of Antilochos,
> Nestor's son, and strong Eumelos drew next after him,
> and after him the son of Atreus, Menelaos the spear-famed.

32

Meriones drew the next lane to drive, and the last for the driving
of horses was drawn by far the best of them all, Diomedes.
They stood in line for the start, and Achilleus showed them the
     turn-post
far away on the level plain, and beside it he stationed
a judge, Phoinix the godlike, the follower of his father,
to mark and remember the running and bring back a true story.

Iliad 23.352–61

The makeshift course is quite simple: once around a turning-post which
Achilles has designated (actually a tree stump standing alone in the Trojan
plain, 23.327) and back to the starting-point. Phoinix is stationed at the
turning-post to report any infractions of the rules. The race is uneventful, if
hotly contested, until the back stretch, when the ever-meddlesome gods start
to wreak havoc. Athena breaks Eumelos' chariot yoke, sending him sprawling and allowing Diomedes to take the lead. Meanwhile, Antilochos reck-
lessly cuts off Menelaos at a narrow patch of the course, moving into second
place. At this point the chariots begin to come back into the view of the
spectators as they enter the final stretch:

Now the Argives who sat in their assembly were watching
the horses, and the horses flew through the dust of the flat land.
Idomeneus, lord of the Kretans, was first to make out the horses,
for he sat apart from the others assembled, and higher up, where
he could see all ways, and from far off he heard Diomedes
calling, and knew him, and made out one horse ahead of the others
who was conspicuous, all red, except on his forehead
there was a white mark, round, like the full moon. Idomeneus
rose to his feet upright and spoke his word out to the Argives:
"Friends, who are leaders of the Argives and keep their counsel:
am I the only one who can see the horses, or can you
also? It seems to me there are other horses leading
and I make out another charioteer."

Iliad 23.448–60

An altercation flares up between two spectators, there is brief talk of a wager
(what else would racing fans do?), and just at that point Diomedes crosses
the finish-line first:

The horses came in running hard. Diomedes stopped them
in the middle of where the men were assembled, with the dense sweat
     starting
and dripping to the ground from neck and chest of his horses.
He himself vaulted down to the ground from his shining chariot
and leaned his whip against the yoke. Nor did strong Sthenelos

Figure 18 Chariot race at the funeral games for Patroklos. Upper frieze of Attic dinos, by Sophilos. Athens, National Museum 15499. Ca. 580–570.

> delay, but made haste to take up the prizes, and gave the woman
> to his high-hearted companions to lead away and the tripod
> with ears to carry, while Diomedes set free the horses.
>
> *Iliad* 23.506–13

The allocation of the remaining prizes proves to be anything but straight-forward, not only owing to the fierce competitiveness of the contestants, but also to an uncharacteristically soft-hearted gesture on Achilles' part, wanting to award the second-prize mare to the last-place Eumelos out of sympathy for his accident. The scene briefly threatens to turn into a hopeless muddle.

It is hardly surprising that on the few occasions when Greek artists wanted to illustrate the games for Patroklos, they focused on the chariot race, to the exclusion of all other events. The subject is limited, quite inexplicably, to a few vases of the early years of Attic black-figure, ca. 575–550, then disappears for good.

Sophilos, the first real personality of black-figure, put the scene on a dinos, a big round punchbowl that was found in a tomb at Pharsalos in Thessaly, where five centuries later Julius Caesar would defeat Pompey the Great (Fig. 18). The site is not far from the Homeric Phthia, whence Achilles and Patroklos came to Troy.

The uppermost frieze of the dinos, a 360° circle uninterrupted by handles, was an ideal surface on which to spread out the coursing chariots of this famous race. Our fragment represents no more than perhaps one-quarter of

34

the original composition, but it is at least in one sense a lucky break, since two key inscriptions are preserved in their entirety: Sophilos' signature as painter and his title for the picture, "Patroklous Atla" (Games [in honor] of Patroklos). The temporary stands from which the spectators observe the race are a curious, ziggurat-like affair. Half watch the team about to gallop by, while the other half look to the chariot in the lead. Among the latter group is Achilles himself, for an inscription naming him is preserved, although not the figure. Instead of comprising only one lap out and back, this race seems to run a circular course, with the horses running so close to the stands that some excited fans can almost reach out and touch them. Particularly effective is the topmost spectator, who has turned back to see the approaching team and will now swivel his head round to follow its course. The name of this team's driver was inscribed, ending in -os (Antilochos?).

A few years after Sophilos, the painter Kleitias, who borrowed several subjects from his older colleague, included this same race on his masterpiece, the volute-krater known as the François Vase (Figs. 19 and 20). But the composition, dictated in part by the narrow, linear strip available to Kleitias, is entirely different. The spectators have been eliminated, all but Achilles, who stands, presumably, at the finish-line, beside one of the prizes, a bronze tripod. The turning-post (not a tree, but a man-made pillar) stands at the far left; we may imagine that all five chariots have made the turn and now come down the final stretch. The evenly spaced chariots conveniently and pleasingly fill the space, but convey little of the chaotic struggle Homer describes. More prizes, cauldrons and tripods, are placed at intervals – not that they are meant to form an obstacle course for the horses, but are simply displayed to remind us of the rich rewards at stake. For this event Achilles did in fact offer an "eared tripod" as first prize (together with a slave-woman) and an "unfired cauldron" as third prize. "Eared" is of course a reference to the big ring-handles soldered onto the rim of the bowl.

Both objects continued to be awarded in athletic contests well into the Archaic and Classical period; this probably accounts for their prominence here more than strict fidelity to the text. After all, Kleitias' choice of names for the contestants betrays either a very faulty memory of the *Iliad* or a conscious choice to follow a different version of the story. Only one of the five, Diomedes, matches Homer's account. The winner appears to be Odysseus (here written as an Archaic variant of his name, "Olyteus"), who is never mentioned by Homer in connection with this race. Yet his reputation as a multi-talented winner in everything from the foot-race later the same day (23.778–79) to the fateful contest for the arms of Achilles (see below, Chapter 4) was so powerful that his intrusion here is easily understandable.

These are the only two representations generally acknowledged to show the games for Patroklos, but a third may with reasonable certainty be added (Figs. 21 and 22). It is on one side of an amphora belonging to the so-called Tyrrhenian group, made in a large workshop in Attica for export to Etruria. The Etruscan clientele who took these vases to their graves were great

Figure 19 Middle: chariot race at the funeral games for Patroklos. *Below*: the wedding of Peleus and Thetis. Attic black-figure volute-krater ("François Vase"), by Kleitias. Florence, Museo Nazionale 4209. Ca. 570–560.

Figure 20 Middle: Achilles watching the chariot race. *Below*: the wedding of Peleus and Thetis. Detail of François Vase shown in Fig. 19 (above).

Figures 21 and 22 Chariot race at the funeral games for Patroklos. Black-figure neck-amphora of the Tyrrhenian Group. Florence, Museo Nazionale 3773. Ca. 560.

37

aficionados of Greek myth and avid fans of Homer and the Epic Cycle. Our scene has no inscriptions to prove which chariot race the painter had in mind, only some strong indications. The stepped bleachers recall those on Sophilos' dinos – only these are more hastily drawn – while the eared tripod and the cauldron (sitting atop the turning-post) are the very prizes shown on the François Vase. The most striking detail, however, is the rear chariot that has come unyoked, sending the driver and one horse crashing to the ground. This can only be the chariot of Eumelos, when Athena sabotaged his car and he "was sent spinning out beside the wheel of the chariot so that his elbows were all torn, and his mouth and his nostrils and his forehead were lacerated about the brows" (23.394–96). The other teams quickly pass him, and, as we see here, he is lucky to avoid being trampled in their wake. The only noticeable departure from Homer is the reduction of the chariots to three, occasioned by limitations of space.

Book 24: Priam and Achilles (the ransom of Hektor)

Once the funeral games are over, Achilles, who had briefly found solace from his grief in playing the generous host, returns to venting his wrath on Hektor's corpse, until his mother brings the command from Zeus to cease and desist. Achilles is thus forewarned that he can expect a visit from Priam, while the Trojan king, for his part, receives divine assurance of safe passage to Achilles' tent for himself and a single old herald, Idaios, with the guidance of Hermes. There is by now no question but that Achilles will return the body of Hektor, yet even so it is appropriate that Priam bring rich gifts to support his entreaty. As Sir Moses Finley once pointed out, a central paradox of Homeric society is that treasure (i.e. precious metals, woven or embroidered textiles, and the like) exists mainly to be given away, on innumerable occasions, as a token of honor and esteem. Thus Priam prepares for the journey:

> He spoke, and lifted back the fair covering of his clothes-chest
> and from inside took out twelve robes surpassingly lovely
> and twelve mantles to be worn single, as many blankets,
> as many great white cloaks, also the same number of tunics.
> He weighed and carried out ten full talents of gold, and brought forth
> two shining tripods, and four cauldrons, and brought out a goblet
> of surpassing loveliness that the men of Thrace had given him
> when he went to them with a message, but now the old man spared not
> even this in his halls, so much was it his heart's desire
> to ransom back his beloved son.
>
> *Iliad* 24.228–37

Priam's departure from Troy is accompanied by great lamentation, above all from his wife Hecuba, who, all the gods' assurances notwithstanding, fears he is headed straight into the jaws of the lion. Idaios drives a mule-cart piled high with the gifts, and Priam follows in his chariot. Escorted by Hermes, in the guise of a young nobleman, they reach the Myrmidons' camp, where Hermes keeps the guards asleep until Priam has arrived at Achilles' chamber. Leaving the party inside the gate, Hermes departs for Olympos, and Priam prepares to face Achilles alone:

> The old man made straight for the dwelling
> where Achilleus the beloved of Zeus was sitting. He found him
> inside, and his companions were sitting apart, as two only,
> Automedon the hero and Alkimos, scion of Ares,
> were busy beside him. He had just now got through with his dinner,
> with eating and drinking, and the table still stood by. Tall Priam
> came in unseen by the other men and stood close beside him
> and caught the knees of Achilleus in his arms, and kissed the hands
> that were dangerous and manslaughtering and had killed so many
> of his sons.
>
> *Iliad* 24.471–80

This is surely a dramatic high-point of the *Iliad*, although more will follow in this remarkable scene. Yet it was this very moment, Priam's entrance before Achilles as a suppliant, on which visual artists almost invariably focused. Unlike most of the scenes we have considered up to this point, the ransom of Hektor had a long lifespan in Greek art and was treated in several periods of vase-painting from the early sixth century until well into the fourth.

A black-figure hydria of about 570 is probably our earliest complete depiction (Fig. 23). Athenian artists of this generation, who included Sophilos and Kleitias (see Figs. 18–20), often had no visual models to rely on and were essentially inventing iconographies as they went along. These early efforts therefore have a particular fascination and often contain imaginative elements that will have disappeared once a scene is "canonized" a generation or two later.

The majestic and forbidding figure of Achilles, reclining on his couch, dominates the middle of the picture. Priam enters with hands outstretched, as we would expect, but his awkward, lunging movement suggests that he is about to throw himself on the ground, unlike the Homeric Priam, who remains dignified and erect. The pose also makes the white-haired and white-bearded old man look even smaller in comparison to the powerful Achilles. Hermes, seated on a small block at the entrance to the tent, thrusts out one hand, as if giving the nervous suppliant the last little push. His presence and lively gesture here, at a moment when Hermes has, strictly speaking, already left the earth, are the kind of liberties we have come to expect vase-painters to take for the sake of clarity and completeness. Likewise, this Hermes is very obviously Hermes, with traveling cap and kerykeion, for gods disguised as mortals do not translate well into visual terms when ease of recognition is the artist's primary goal.

Figure 23 The ransom of Hektor. Attic black-figure hydria, attributed to the Painter of London B76. Zurich University (on loan). Ca. 570–560.

Alongside Achilles' couch is a table with the remains of his dinner, long strips of meat. A second, lower table behind him holds a full set of armor which must be Hektor's, since his corpse is stretched out below it. Here the painter has indulged his imagination, for Homer makes no mention of Hektor's armor, much less says that it was so prominently displayed. Yet it is a detail fully in keeping with the spirit of the *Iliad*, in which so much importance is attached to the taking of enemy armor. Ironically, this set of armor was originally Achilles' own, for at his death Hektor was wearing the borrowed armor that he had stripped from the body of Patroklos.

Placing the corpse so near to Achilles, where Priam cannot fail to see it, is also an unhomeric touch, yet one that becomes indispensable in every painted version of this scene. Indeed, in Homer, Achilles goes to great pains *not* to let Priam see the corpse, even loading it himself onto the cart. The dog sleeping under Achilles' couch surely has more to do with the painter's need to fill every available space than with a grim parody of the corpse of Hektor nearby.

From the perspective of later depictions of this subject, the painter of the Zurich vase is equally eccentric for what he adds (the table with Hektor's armor) as for what he leaves out. In particular, he omits any reference to the

40

rich gifts Priam has brought, although these will soon become a central element of the scene. A half-century after the hydria, another black-figure painter gives us what have become all the key ingredients, compressed into the nearly square panel of a belly-amphora (Fig. 24). Priam's gesture of supplication, with outstretched arms, is similar, and we can easily imagine that he will take hold of, even kiss, Achilles' murderous hands. What the painters never managed to capture is the still more Homeric token of supplication, clasping the knees. In this scene, as in most others, it was precluded by Achilles' reclining position, in which his knees disappear under a mass of drapery. Hektor's corpse has now assumed its standard position, directly under Achilles' couch, and the armor has been hung up on the tent's inside wall.

Priam is accompanied by a servant-boy carrying the first load of ransom, a bronze tripod and three metal phialai neatly stacked. Homer has Achilles himself, with two henchmen, fetch the treasure Priam has left outside the tent (24.572–81), but the painter's solution is much more effective in showing the necessary link between supplication and gifts. The tripod, already familiar to us as a prize (see Figs. 20, 22), is equally suitable for all types of gift exchange, and the phialai could represent the ten talents' weight of gold that Priam brought. A curious detail is the matching phiale in Achilles' hand, held out so ostentatiously, as if to say he has no need of Priam's gifts; but

Figure 24 The ransom of Hektor. Attic black-figure amphora, attributed to Rycroft Painter. Toledo, Museum of Art 72.54. Ca. 520.

41

more likely his phiale is either a practical touch (Achilles had just been dining, drinking his wine from this cup) or simply a standard element in the iconography of the reclining hero in Archaic art.

Hermes is a dapper figure, with wings on his cap as well as his boots. He is balanced, behind Achilles, by a woman holding a large water-jar, or hydria. In such a carefully planned composition, one is reluctant to dismiss her as a "filler," but what could the artist have had in mind? It has been suggested that the hydria is part of the ransom, one not mentioned by Homer, or that she is Briseis. Might she not better be one of the servant-girls Achilles summoned to wash Hektor's corpse (24.581–83), carrying water for the task?

In the heyday of Late Archaic red-figure, about 500–480, the ransom of Hektor allowed vase-painters to indulge their taste for both emotional power and the pomp and splendor of the heroic past. No version gives us such ample measure of both these qualities as a cup now in a private collection in New York. By spreading the scene over both sides of the exterior (Figs. 25 and 26), the painter has turned a formerly intimate scene into a grand and stately procession. In Priam and Achilles, the contrast of youth and age that was so effective on the Toledo amphora (and will be so important to Homer as the scene unfolds) is enhanced by a new element, a contrast between the relaxed, elegantly coiffed young hero and the timid and humbled old man. Priam's stubbly beard and sparse hair may allude, however discreetly, to the fact that he has spent much of his time since Hektor's death wallowing in mud and dung (24.163–65) and has not slept for days. Again a woman stands behind Achilles, but this time the wreath that she holds out to Achilles suggests that she is none other than Briseis, now returned to Achilles' tent. Later that evening she will join him in bed (24.676).

In Homer, Achilles has finished his meal when Priam arrives, but our painter has altered this a little, putting in the hero's hands a piece of meat and an uncomfortably large knife. One cannot help but suspect that this conspicuous weapon has more than culinary significance, for Achilles brandishes it just as Priam reaches ever so tentatively to touch him. Beside underscoring Achilles' position of authority and power, the knife is a perfect visual metaphor for another of Achilles' traits, his razor-sharp, hair-trigger temper. Priam will shortly get a taste of this, when Achilles feels he is being pressured to release the body too quickly and reacts with surprising vehemence: "no longer stir me up, old sir . . . for I fear I might not let you alone in my shelter, suppliant as you are" (24.560–70).

Hermes once again remains in the tent, but now takes on a new function, directing the large contingent of Priam's attendants who will carry in the ransom. A pair of columns, one on each side of the vase, indicate that these bearers are still outside the tent proper, although inside the door to the compound which is indicated behind the last of the procession. This large

Figure 25 The ransom of Hektor (Priam before Achilles). Attic red-figure cup, attributed to the Painter of the Fourteenth Brygos, side A. New York, Collection of Shelby White and Leon Levy. Ca. 480.

Figure 26 Ransom brought to Achilles' tent. Side B of the cup shown in Fig. 25 (above).

43

Figure 27 Priam and Achilles. Interior of the cup shown in Fig. 25 (p. 43).

retinue is, of course, a blatant violation of Zeus' strict orders to Priam, to go alone to Achilles' tent, save for the old herald (24.148–49), yet it is the only way the painter knew to show off the rich gifts. A thousand years earlier, in Egypt and Crete, such processions of tribute-bearers were already a well established motif. The ransom itself here bears even less relation to Homer's catalog than in earlier versions: a full set of armor, metal vessels in all shapes and sizes, from dinos and hydria to phialai and pointed amphora, a footbath, and even a glass perfume-jar. Nowhere in evidence are the piles of textiles to which Homer gives priority.

Inside the cup (Fig. 27), Priam and Achilles continue their dialog on a more intimate basis. This is not simply an excerpt from the larger scene on the exterior, for the corpse has been removed so as not to upset Priam or provoke Achilles to anger (cf. 24.583–85). This is a true narrative sequence, one of the boldest such experiments in the art of the period. The painter was well aware that the interview of Priam and Achilles did not end with that first exchange. It would be a breach of Homeric etiquette if the visitor were not invited to share a meal, especially in this instance when, as Achilles suspects, the grieving Priam has not eaten for several days (24.641–42). For Achilles this means a second huge meal when he has barely had time to digest the first, but such are the constraints of hospitality.

In other respects, too, the quiet scene in the tondo is far from a repeat of the outside. The two men look each other straight in the eye: "Priam, son of Dardanos, gazed upon Achilles, wondering at his size and beauty, for he seemed like an outright vision of gods. Achilles in turn gazed on Dardanian Priam and wondered" (24.629–32). As Achilles looks on the broken old man, he thinks of his own father, Peleus, back in Greece, whom he will never see again. It is a moment of ineffable sadness that the painter can only intimate in his silent dialog.

The pathos is almost unbearable, but never maudlin. For Homer always reminds us that life goes on and so does the war. Thus Achilles briskly informs Priam that he and the herald will sleep outside the tent, on the porch, lest some of Achilles' men burst in during the night and recognize Priam (24.650–55). Hermes is likewise worried about how best to smuggle Priam out of the Greek camp and so rouses the king while it is still dark. The concluding scene of the *Iliad*, the lamentation over the body of Hektor in Troy, soon follows. Achilles will not live long after the death of Hektor; this he has known all along. But for Homer this is less important than the spiritual transformation he has undergone in those few quiet moments with Priam in the tent. He has laid to rest the implacable wrath that consumed him since the opening of the poem and so achieved his greatest heroic stature.

HOMER'S *ODYSSEY*: THE WANDERINGS AND HOMECOMING OF ODYSSEUS

The poem we know as the *Odyssey* was once part of a larger cycle under the general title *Nostoi* (Returns), telling how the various Greek heroes made their way home from Troy and what they found when they got there. The *Odyssey* is the only poem of this cycle to survive, because it was the only one believed to be a genuine work of Homer. One of the now lost epics told the story of Agamemnon's homecoming and murderous reception by his unfaithful wife Klytaimestra, best known to us from Aeschylus' *Oresteia* (see Chapter 4). This cautionary tale offered a perfect counterpoint to Odysseus' experience, the faithful Penelope vs. the shameless Klytaimestra, as Homer himself often observes (e.g. *Odyssey* 11.405–57). While Agamemnon's journey home into the snares of death took only a few days, the same trip took Odysseus ten years. The *Odyssey* does not tell the story of these ten years in any straightforward chronological sequence. It is part of Homer's genius to begin the poem in the last of those ten years and then narrate the earlier adventures in extended flashbacks, mostly in Odysseus' own voice.

The setting is the island of the Phaeacians, where Odysseus is wined and dined and, in return, entertains his hosts with spellbinding tales of high adventure and narrow escapes; but how he got to this fairy-tale island and won the favor of its xenophobic people constitutes one of the most subtle triumphs of this "man of many wiles."

Book 6: Odysseus and Nausikaa

For seven years, Odysseus had been a "prisoner" of the beautiful nymph Kalypso, forced to make love to her but – if we are to believe Homer – all the while pining for his wife and home on Ithaca. At Athena's behest, he is finally released and sets out on a simple raft outfitted with a sail. (Only later will we learn how it is that Odysseus is by now utterly alone, having lost his entire crew in one mishap or another.) As so often before, Poseidon will not let Odysseus travel the sea unimpeded, but sends wind and waves to wreck the raft and plunge Odysseus into the roiling water. A kindly sea-nymph named Ino, or Leukothea, rescues him with advice to abandon the raft and swim for shore, and with the gift of a magic veil that will insure he does not drown. Washed ashore on Scheria (the Phaeacians' island), he is once again in the familiar situation of having no idea where he is. After narrowly escaping the deadly rocks of the jagged coast, he reaches the mouth of a gentle river, gathers a bed of leaves, protected from the wind and frost by some bushes, and collapses in exhaustion.

Next morning his sleep is pierced by the shrill cries of young girls. Nausikaa, teenage daughter of the island's king, Alkinoos, had come down to the river with her companions to do the laundry and enjoy a picnic by the river. Once the clothes have been laid out to dry on the rocks, the girls are at play when their ball lands in the water, occasioning the cries that awaken Odysseus. He stirs from the underbrush, wondering to himself what sort of people (or nymphs?) he is about to encounter:

> So speaking, great Odysseus came from under his thicket,
> and from the dense foliage with his heavy hand he broke off
> a leafy branch to cover his body and hide the male parts,
> and went in the confidence of his strength, like some hill-kept lion,
> who advances, though he is rained on and blown by the wind, and both eyes
> kindle; he goes out after cattle or sheep, or it may be
> deer in the wilderness, and his belly is urgent upon him
> to get inside of a close steading and go for the sheepflocks.
> So Odysseus was ready to face young girls with well-ordered
> hair, naked though he was, for the need was on him; and yet
> he appeared terrifying to them, all crusted with dry spray,
> and they scattered one way and another down the jutting beaches.
> Only the daughter of Alkinoös stood fast, for Athene
> put courage into her heart, and took the fear from her body,
> and she stood her ground and faced him, and now Odysseus debated

46

whether to supplicate the well-favored girl by clasping
her knees, or stand off where he was and in words of blandishment
ask if she would show him the city, and lend him clothing.
Then in the division of his heart this way seemed best to him,
to stand well off and supplicate in words of blandishment,
for fear that, if he clasped her knees, the girl might be angry.
So blandishingly and full of craft he began to address her.

Odyssey 6.127–48

The witty charm of this episode and the brilliant psychological portrait of the adolescent Nausikaa were beyond the powers of any ancient artist to capture, and most wisely did not try. Two red-figure vases of the Classical period, however, do have an amusing charm of their own, not least in the sometimes startling liberties they take with Homer's text. A large neck-amphora of about 440 covers the whole surface with the story (Fig. 28). A learned German scholar of the nineteenth century, who produced the first publication of the vase, was so distressed by its many departures from Homer's text that he suggested the painter must have been a non-Greek immigrant in Athens. There are indeed details one could quibble with, such as the scrawny branches that fail miserably to cover Odysseus' nakedness, or the laundry hanging in the tree when it should be drying on the rocks; but two key elements indicate that the painter was not so much ignorant of the text as pursuing his own narrative agenda.

First, the ball-game has been entirely suppressed and much detail instead lavished on the wringing-out of the wet laundry, which was long since finished when Odysseus made his appearance. Second, the goddess Athena

Figure 28 Odysseus and Nausikaa. Attic red-figure neck-amphora, attributed to the Nausikaa Painter (name vase). Munich, Antikensammlungen 2322. Ca. 440.

has suddenly materialized, firmly planted between Odysseus and the girls (she in fact occupies the exact center of the front side of the vase).

A few years before the date of this vase, Sophocles had presented a play on the subject, entitled *Nausikaa* or *The Washer Women*. It was clearly the laundry that best conjured up the story in the popular imagination, as it still does today, so the vase-painter "adjusts" the timing to preserve this motif. Hanging in the tree, the laundry is, of course, also much more evident to the viewer than it would be if spread on the ground.

Athena is a different matter, not so much a rearranging of the text as the making visible of a notion well grounded in the text, that Athena has engineered this entire episode. It was she who put the idea in Nausikaa's head (in a dream) to go down to the river, and it is she who gives Nausikaa the courage to stand her ground when the other girls run; and in the next scene she will magically beautify and rejuvenate Odysseus for his entry into Phaeacia town. In her stately grandeur, she is a divine epiphany, not even visible to the mortal actors, but only to us.

It is evident by now that the painter's principal goal was narrative clarity,

Figure 29 Odysseus and Nausikaa. Attic red-figure pyxis lid, attributed to Aison. Boston, Museum of Fine Arts 04.18. Ca. 430.

bringing together all the most easily recognizable ingredients in a simple, paratactic composition. Only one element is left frustratingly vague: we cannot tell who is Nausikaa. She *should* be the girl nearest Odysseus, but why then does she look as if she is turning to flee? Nor is she distinguished from her companions in size or beauty, as Homer would have us believe (6.101–9). We can only think that the painter was not really interested in her; for him the story is about Odysseus.

There is no such difficulty recognizing Nausikaa on the second red-figure scene (Fig. 29), about a decade later, where her identity is, if anything, overdetermined. Not only does she stand calm and coolly aloof as her two companions flee hysterically (the third is so engrossed in her washing that she has not noticed Odysseus' approach), but, like the others, her name is inscribed. As Nausikaa's nonchalant posture is wonderfully expressive, so too is Odysseus', as he crouches in modesty and trepidation. Wound around his arm and shoulder is the veil of Ino/Leukothea. He had, in fact, returned the veil to the sea by now (5.459–62), as the nymph instructed him – perhaps this is a pedantic touch of the painter, to remind us how Odysseus got here. This same fastidiousness is evident in the bits of applied clay along the ground level, pebbles marking the bank of the river, as well as in the names given to Nausikaa's companions, who remain anonymous in Homer.

However, if Aison wants to show us how well he knows his *Odyssey*, in his Athena he seems to be trying to outdo Homer. No longer an unseen epiphany, she takes charge of the scene with a purposeful look toward Odysseus and a commanding gesture, as if afraid he might start to supplicate the wrong girl. This is truly the Homeric Athena, pulling all the strings and leaving nothing to chance.

Book 9: the blinding of Polyphemos and the escape from the cave

Led by Nausikaa, Odysseus makes his way to the palace of her parents and wins their hospitality. His true identity, as so often in the poem, is concealed for some time and only revealed after a long evening's banquet. Although the hour is late, Odysseus launches into an account of his many wanderings since sailing from Troy nearly ten years before. One of the early stops was a land inhabited by Cyclopes, huge, solitary cave-dwellers marked by a single eye in the middle of the brow.

Odysseus had chosen a dozen of his best men to accompany him in exploring the Cyclops Polyphemos' cave while its proprietor was out tending his flocks and, more out of curiosity than anything else, in waiting there for his return. This was, of course, a mistake, for the Cyclops immediately seals his cave with a massive boulder, trapping the men inside. His first response to Odysseus' plea for hospitality is to snatch up two of the men, dash their brains out, and eat them for dinner. The gruesome meal is repeated the next day, but Odysseus has hit upon a stratagem: to sharpen a length of olive wood found lying in the cave and harden it in the fire. As the Cyclops prepares his third Greek meal, Odysseus offers him a cup of strong, sweet wine that he has brought along from the ship. Well pleased, the Cyclops accepts several more draughts of wine:

> He spoke and slumped away and fell on his back, and lay there
> with his thick neck crooked over on one side, and sleep who subdues
>   all
> came on and captured him, and the wine gurgled up from his gullet
> with gobs of human meat. This was his drunken vomiting.
> Then I shoved the beam underneath a deep bed of cinders,
> waiting for it to heat, and I spoke to all my companions
> in words of courage, so none should be in a panic, and back out;
> but when the beam of olive, green as it was, was nearly
> at the point of catching fire and glowed, terribly incandescent,
> then I brought it close up from the fire and my friends about me
> stood fast. Some great divinity breathed courage into us.
> They seized the beam of olive, sharp at the end, and leaned on it
> into the eye, while I from above leaning my weight on it
> twirled it, like a man with a brace-and-bit who bores into
> a ship timber, and his men from underneath, grasping
> the strap on either side whirl it, and it bites resolutely deeper.
> So seizing the fire-point-hardened timber we twirled it
> in his eye, and the blood boiled around the hot point, so that
> the blast and scorch of the burning ball singed all his eyebrows
> and eyelids, and the fire made the roots of his eye crackle.
> As when a man who works as a blacksmith plunges a screaming
> great ax blade or plane into cold water, treating it
> for temper, since this is the way steel is made strong, even
> so Cyclops' eye sizzled about the beam of the olive.
>
> *Odyssey* 9.371–94

Earlier, Odysseus had said he picked four of the men to help him drive the stake into Polyphemos' eye (6.335). It is not clear if any of these was eaten before the blinding, but in any case there can only be six men left beside Odysseus. Their lives are still imperiled, for although the blinded Cyclops has removed the boulder to let out the sheep, he guards the entrance to the cave to catch any Greek who tries to escape. A second stratagem is needed:

> There were some male sheep, rams, well nourished, thick and fleecy,
> handsome and large, with a dark depth of wool. Silently
> I caught these and lashed them together with pliant willow
> withes, where the monstrous Cyclops lawless of mind had used to
> sleep. I had them in threes, and the one in the middle carried
> a man, while the other two went on each side, so guarding
> my friends. Three rams carried each man, but as for myself,

there was one ram, far the finest of all the flock. This one
I clasped around the back, snuggled under the wool of the belly,
and stayed there still, and with a firm twist of the hands and enduring
spirit clung fast to the glory of this fleece, unrelenting.

Odyssey 9.425–35

The episode, comprising two key moments, the blinding and the escape, must have caught the imagination of people all over the Mediterranean, for it appears in the art of a variety of regions, starting at a date astonishingly soon after the composition of the *Odyssey* ca. 700 B.C. Although details vary, there is enough consistency – especially in view of the geographical range – to suggest that all the artists were inspired by the Homeric poem.

The earliest of these, working in Attica about 670, produced for a child's burial at Eleusis one of the most magnificent examples of the so-called Orientalizing style (Figs. 30 and 31). His imaginative approach to mythological narration is borne out by the complex scene of Perseus fleeing the Gorgons on the belly of this huge amphora. For the neck he chose the blinding of Polyphemos, a subject not especially well suited to this fairly narrow surface. Yet in one respect the artist has made a virtue of a necessity: the compression of the figures in a tight space effectively conveys the claustrophobic feeling of the cave. Odysseus' companions have been reduced from four to two, and he is surely the forward-most, singled out by his white body while all the others are in black silhouette. In this cramped space, the Cyclops is forced to sit upright, instead of sprawling in his drunken stupor, but this too has happy consequences: his body is so huge that the men must stand on tiptoe and hold the pole over their heads just to reach the level of his eye. Especially effective is Odysseus' pose, kicking out one leg in order to give that extra bit of momentum to the desperate thrust.

The Cyclops' mouth is wide open: "He gave a giant horrible cry and the rocks rattled to the sound" (9.395–96). With one hand he tries vainly to ward off the pole, while the other still holds the wine cup that was his undoing. In all respects this Cyclops is far more alert and awake than Homer's drunken, sleeping victim. The helplessness, which in the poem works to create a curious sympathy for the monster, is here diminished in favor of the heroism of Odysseus and his men.

Although Polyphemos is always depicted with superhuman proportions, few later artists would ever capture his massive size and bulk as effectively as the Polyphemos Painter at Eleusis. On a cup made in Sparta over a century later, for example, the seated Cyclops comes up to the level of Odysseus and his men, who shoulder the pole without much enthusiasm (Fig. 32). What lends the scene its naïve charm is the pair of human legs the Cyclops holds, the remnants of his last meal. Like the wine cup, they violate the integrity of the myth, which requires the Cyclops to be asleep, or at least passed out. The painter's approach to narrative is almost childlike in its simplicity: he

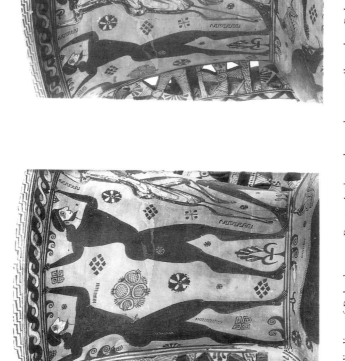

Figures 30 and 31 Blinding of Polyphemos. Proto-Attic neck-amphora, attributed to Polyphemos Painter (name vase). Eleusis. Ca. 670–660.

Figure 32 Blinding of Polyphemos. Laconian cup attributed to the Rider Painter, interior. Paris, Cabinet des Médailles 190. Ca. 550. After K. Schefold, *Götter- und Heldensagen der Griechen in der spätarchaischen Kunst* (Munich, 1978) 269, fig. 353.

combines all the elements of the episode in an impossible moment that becomes a kind of emblem of the story rather than the story itself. His lack of interest in Homer's text is evident in other details as well. Odysseus is hard to pick out: he is either the youth proffering the cup to Polyphemos or, more likely, the one bearded figure bringing up the rear. This Cyclops evidently has two eyes, for the stake goes not into the left eye, which we see, but the right, which we do not. Lastly, there are the animals, a snake winding its way, with open jaws, toward the Cyclops and a big fish chasing a dotted circle in the exergue. There is no point in looking in Homer for clues to their meaning. Comparison with other Laconian cups would be more fruitful, and reveals that they often add such extraneous elements, especially in the space below the figured scene. The snake, however, is perhaps too much a part of the scene to be so lightly dismissed. As he parallels the deadly pole and moves perilously close to the Cyclops' face, it is probably not too far-fetched to see him as a kind of visual simile for the sneak attack. At any rate, he gives the scene a little frisson of horror that the listless Greeks and immobilized Cyclops fail to provide.

To find a truly unfettered interpretation of the Polyphemos episode in the visual arts, we must turn to Athens in the period of early black-figure. On a cup of the mid-sixth century, the subject is really how the Cyclops was made drunk, and there is no sign of the instrument of his blinding (Fig. 33). Indeed, there is some doubt as to whether this artist had in mind the blinding at all, since two of Odysseus' men watch with drawn swords. Odysseus had briefly considered plunging his sword into the Cyclops, then realized that the monster's death would leave him and his men trapped forever in the cave, unable to move the boulder that sealed it (6.298–305). In any case, these men do not look as if they are about to attack the Cyclops, but only defend themselves should the wine not take effect; but the wine *is* taking effect, as we can see from the ungainly pose into which the massive Cyclops is sinking. It is a great pity that a large chunk of the bowl is missing, including his head and that of Odysseus; but we can be fairly certain that it showed Odysseus offering a cup of wine in one hand while holding back the wine jug in the other. The big wineskin held at the ready by one of the men is a nice touch that does not occur elsewhere. One would especially like to see how Polyphemos' face and head were rendered, for there are indications in what is preserved that his barbarism was imaginatively caricatured: the massive belly and the large, fat penis, always a token in Greek art of bestiality and lack of decency. Perhaps most interesting is the sudden appearance of Athena, fully armed, to lend moral support to her protégé. Needless to say, no Greek viewer imagined that Athena actually accompanied Odysseus into the Cyclops' cave. This is, rather, one of the earliest instances of the kind of divine epiphany we have already observed in Classical art (see Fig. 28).

The escape from the cave of Polyphemos enjoys a popularity in Greek vase-painting that closely parallels that of the blinding, from Proto-Attic of the mid-seventh century to the Late Archaic of about 500. We may single out one representation which, although fragmentary, preserves one of the most splendid Cyclopes we have (Fig. 34). It comes from the rim of a volute-

Figure 33 Polyphemos made drunk with Odysseus' wine. Attic black-figure cup attributed to the Painter of the Boston Polyphemos (name vase). Boston, Museum of Fine Arts 99.518. Ca. 550.

Figure 34 Escape of Odysseus from the cave of Polyphemos. Fragment of volute-krater, attributed to Kleitias. Basel, Collection of Herbert Cahn. Ca. 570–560.

krater by Kleitias that must once have rivaled the brilliance, if not the size, of the François Vase (cf. Figs. 19 and 20). One other surviving fragment of this vase continues the story of Perseus and the Gorgons, of which we see one figure on the Cahn fragment, below the ram. Polyphemos is indeed blind, as indicated by a jagged slit where his eye should be. His bestiality is now suggested in new and different ways whose inspiration comes not from Homer but rather from the conventions of early black-figure: the long hair flowing down the back, thick body hair rendered by incision (as also on satyrs of this period), and added red pigment for the face, a rare and peculiar trait that seems to mark creatures who are neither human nor divine. His hands, groping for the last ram as it carries Odysseus to safety, convey his sightlessness even more effectively than the missing eye. This ram is, of course, the leader of the flock, the one that Odysseus chose for himself because of its extra-thick fleece. The long narrow rim of this krater had space for all Odysseus' surviving companions. One would like to know if the artful Kleitias reproduced the one Homeric detail that no other painter remembered, the three rams lashed together to conceal each of the other men (9.429–30).

Book 10: Circe

The adventure in the Cyclops' cave cost the lives of six of Odysseus' men. This was a small toll compared to that exacted soon after by the Laistrygones, another race of man-eating monsters. No sooner had Odysseus' fleet tied up in their harbor than they suddenly appeared *en masse*, pelted the ships with boulders, and killed most of their crews.

Odysseus' ship alone escaped destruction and made landfall next on Aiaia, the island of Circe.

While Odysseus waits by the ship, a contingent of twenty-two men, led by the trusty Eurylochos, goes to investigate Circe's handsome stone house. Before meeting the enchantress herself, they encounter wild lions and wolves which, under her spells, are as gentle as puppy dogs, and they hear Circe's voice as she sings at the loom. She invites them in and welcomes them all with a potion that turns them into pigs – all but Eurylochos, who had prudently waited outside. When Odysseus is informed, he immediately sets out, armed with sword and bow; but ordinary weapons would be powerless against Circe's magic, so Odysseus needs divine assistance, from Hermes. The god provides him with the moly plant, the antidote to Circe's potion. Thus prepared he angrily confronts her:

> She made me sit down in a chair that was wrought elaborately
> and splendid with silver nails, and under my feet was a footstool.
> She made a potion for me to drink and gave it in a golden
> cup, and with evil thoughts in her heart added the drug to it.
> Then when she had given it and I drank it off, without being
> enchanted, she struck me with her wand and spoke and named me:
> "Go to your sty now and lie down with your other friends there."
> So she spoke, but I, drawing from beside my thigh the sharp sword,
> rushed forward against Circe as if I were raging to kill her,
> but she screamed aloud and ran under my guard, and clasping both
> knees
> in loud lamentation spoke to me and addressed me in winged words:
> "What man are you and whence? Where are your city and parents?
> The wonder is on me that you drank my drugs and have not been
> enchanted, for no other man beside could have stood up
> under my drugs, once he drank and they passed the barrier
> of his teeth. There is a mind in you no magic will work on.
> You are then resourceful Odysseus. Argeïphontes
> of the golden staff was forever telling me you would come
> to me, on your way back from Troy with your fast black ship.
> Come then, put away your sword in its sheath, and let us
> two go up into my bed so that, lying together
> in the bed of love, we may then have faith and trust in each other."
>
> *Odyssey* 10.314–35

Throughout the Archaic and Classical periods, this is perhaps the most often depicted of Odyssean stories, at least among Attic vase-painters. There is great variety in their depictions, and it is not always easy to know whether to ascribe this to artistic license or to the influence of rival versions of the myth that must have circulated in oral form and occasionally left traces in later writers. The earliest extant scene decorates the other side of the Boston

56

Polyphemos cup that we have already looked at (Fig. 35). It not only includes a number of these variant elements, but in overall composition presents the "textbook" example of a mode of narrative that appears to be uniquely Archaic.

Circe herself stands in the center, mixing a cup of her special brew. Her magic wand doubles as a kind of swizzle-stick. Her nudity is rather startling and not altogether easy to explain. Surely if the Homeric Circe had appeared at her doorstep in the nude, to invite the men in, this would have merited comment. At this period of Greek art, female nudity is very rare and generally means only one thing: hetairai, or professional prostitutes. The painter, looking ahead, knew that Circe will straightaway take Odysseus to her bed, a gesture of sexual forwardness unthinkable for a respectable Greek woman. Perhaps the nudity was his way of translating that side of her nature into visual terms immediately recognizable to his audience. It was a bold gesture that later painters would not repeat. On the other hand, an equally bold innovation of this scene was to prove extremely influential: the men are only partially metamorphosed, from the chest up, and otherwise remain human. They also keep their human upright posture. At one level, this reflects Greek art's delight in all manner of *Mischwesen* (centaurs and satyrs come first to mind); but it also lends the scene a touch of pathos, for the men are well aware of what has happened to them: "but the minds within them stayed as they had been before" (10.240–41). Instead of all becoming pigs, some have been turned into other creatures: lion, ram, and dog. Although it is true that in Homer this first batch of men are all turned into pigs (10.239–43), there is mention later of the possibility of transformation into

Figure 35 Circe turning Odysseus' men into animals. Side B of the cup shown in Fig. 33 (p. 54).

57

Figures 36 and 37 Odysseus threatening Circe. Attic black-figure lekythos attributed to the Daybreak Painter. Taranto, Museo Nazionale 9125. Ca. 510–500.

wolf or lion (10.433). Is the dog at Circe's feet a Greek who got an extra-strong dose of the potion? I rather think it is simply a dog, and its purpose is to point up a paradox of which Homer was also aware, that, aside from her magic powers and sexual liberation, Circe leads a surprisingly normal domestic life. This is expressed in the poem by her attention to her weaving (10.222–24), the activity most characteristic of respectable housewives, including Odysseus' own wife, Penelope.

Thus far, the scene is a reasonably close rendering of the moment Circe first doles out the potion. But with the addition of two more Greeks, the painter destroys any conventional sense of linear time. The one charging in from the left with drawn sword is, of course, Odysseus, whose entrance is made all the more dramatic as Circe is "caught in the act." This is a relatively minor adjustment to the sequence of events. However, if the man at right, fleeing in distress, is indeed Eurylochos (the only plausible identification),

58

then we have a peculiar telescoping of multiple stages in the story. The effect is a little bit like a French farce, in which one character exits stage-right at the very instant another enters left in impossibly perfect timing. For the artist it meant the ability to transcend the borders of the vase and squeeze an entire episode into an astonishingly small space.

As we have observed several times already, it is the earliest black-figure painters who usually produced the most interesting narratives. By the late sixth century they had all too often settled into a kind of unimaginative conformity. So it is with a lekythos in Taranto, one of several depicting Circe (Figs. 36 and 37). The transformed Greeks are now all pigs, but it is hard to tell if their agitated movements are meant to reflect their mental state or simply suggest that they are frolicking in Circe's yard (indicated by the swirling vines). The nicest touch is the drinking cup that Circe lets slip in her fright as Odysseus charges at her.

Book 22: the slaying of the suitors

The visual tradition was so fixated on the image of Circe as evil sorceress that it barely acknowledges her more important roles later in the poem. At Odysseus' request she cheerfully restores the men to human form (improving them in the process: 10.395–96), then invites them all to share her abundant food and drink for as long as they like. A full year goes by, until the men become impatient and implore Odysseus to leave. His thoughts of home have been banished by his nightly visits to Circe's bed, but the men enjoy no such distraction. At this point, Circe assumes the role of Odysseus' trusted adviser, mapping out for him his descent into the Underworld to consult the seer Teiresias (Book 11), as well as warning him of subsequent perils, including the Sirens, Scylla and Charybdis, and the forbidden cattle of the Sun (Book 12).

The second half of the *Odyssey* is set entirely on Ithaca, and the very gradual working-out of Odysseus' revenge on the suitors and reunion with his family is a masterpiece of Homeric plotting and psychological insights. None of this lends itself easily to visual depiction, and there is only the occasional preserved representation: Eurykleia washing Odysseus' feet (and recognizing the scar); Odysseus and the swineherd Eumaios setting out for the palace. Even the dramatic climax of the poem, the slaughter of the suitors in Odysseus' halls, evoked relatively little interest among the painters. Interestingly, the fullest account of this episode in pre-Hellenistic art is a carved frieze that decorated a small hero-shrine in Lycia, a semi-Hellenized kingdom in Asia Minor.

In the *Odyssey*, the slaughter of the suitors, so long in the planning, is not over in an instant. It stretches out quite realistically over an entire book. There were, after all, over a hundred suitors, of whom not one would survive the carnage (only the musician and the herald are spared). One has the feeling that Homer's listeners wanted to savor every drop of blood and gore. This, however, presented a dilemma for a vase-painter, who could not hope to capture this truly epic mayhem, let alone the considerable suspense that Homer injects, over whether Odysseus can really pull it off, outnumbered as he is. Perhaps the most memorable image of Book 22 is the very first one: Odysseus holding the bow he has just strung and used to fire an arrow through a dozen axe-heads. In an instant, this very bow, that was to decide Penelope's new husband, in the hands of its rightful owner turns into an instrument of mass destruction:

> Now resourceful Odysseus stripped his rags from him, and sprang
> up atop the great threshold, holding his bow and the quiver
> filled with arrows, and scattered out the swift shafts before him
> on the ground next his feet, and spoke his word to the suitors:
> "Here is a task that has been achieved, without any deception.

Now I shall shoot at another mark, one that no man yet
has struck, if I can hit it and Apollo grants me the glory."
    He spoke, and steered a bitter arrow against Antinoös.
He was on the point of lifting up a fine two-handled
goblet of gold, and had it in his hands, and was moving it
so as to drink of the wine, and in his heart there was no thought
of death. For who would think that one man, alone in a company
of many men at their feasting, though he were a very strong one,
would ever inflict death upon him and dark doom? But Odysseus,
aiming at this man, struck him in the throat with an arrow,
and clean through the soft part of the neck the point was driven.
He slumped away to one side, and out of his stricken hand fell
the goblet, and up and through his nostrils there burst a thick jet
of mortal blood, and with a thrust of his foot he kicked back
the table from him, so that all the good food was scattered
on the ground, bread and baked meats together; but all the suitors
clamored about the house when they saw that the man was fallen,
sprang up from their seats and ranged about the room, throwing
their glances every way all along the well-built walls,
but there was never a shield there nor any strong spear for them.

Odyssey 22.1–25

The painter of a red-figure skyphos in about 440 may have had these verses in mind, since Odysseus still fights alone, not yet joined by his son Telemachos or the swineherd (Figs. 38 and 39). One victim has been shot in the back, while another has snatched up a little table as protection, just as one of the suitors advises his friends (22.74). The third, holding his hand out in a pathetic and futile gesture of self-defense, effectively sums up their helpless predicament. Two servant-girls, standing behind Odysseus, look equally distressed, one wringing her hands, the other with hand to cheek as if to say, "Oh my." In fact none of the women in the palace witnessed the slaughter, but by adding them to the scene, the painter surely knew he would evoke a smile of recognition from the viewer. The horror slowly creeping over these girls comes not so much from the slaughter they see before them, but from the realization of what lies in store for them later. The twelve who were disloyal to Odysseus in his absence and slept with the suitors will be strung up in this very room.

    An early Apulian krater, close in style to Attic red-figure but with the wonderfully expressive faces of South Italian, has a lively rendition of the slaughter, now in full swing (Fig. 40). We must imagine Odysseus to have been at the far left of the scene, for the arrows flying thick and fast from his bow all come from that direction. Meanwhile, Telemachos has joined the fray: we see him in hand-to-hand combat with an already wounded, bearded suitor. Others try to defend themselves with anything from a footstool to a

Figure 38 Odysseus and two maids. Attic red-figure skyphos, attributed to the Penelope Painter. Berlin, Pergamon Museum 2588. Ca. 440.

bedspread. One had thought to turn the table into an impromptu weapon, but has been cut down first by an arrow. One conspicuous element of the scene is less indebted to Homer than to the iconographical conventions of the Athenian symposium. The suitors share couches in pairs of bearded man and beardless youth, and most are decked out with wreaths, reflecting the festive mood in the hall that has been so abruptly shattered.

We may compare the momentary snapshots of the slaughter on these Attic and South Italian vases with the version on a Hellenistic relief bowl (see Fig.

Figure 39 The death of the suitors. Side B of the skyphos shown in Fig. 38 (above).

Figure 40 The killing of the suitors. Apulian calyx-krater, fragments, attributed to the Hearst Painter. Basel, Collection of Herbert Cahn. Ca. 400.

3), which struggles to convey the epic sweep of Book 22 on a humble vessel. The several episodes, each combined with the appropriate excerpt from the text, seem almost randomly chosen, except that the unfolding frieze begins and ends with the same figure, the traitorous goatherd Melanthios.

Like the *Iliad*, the *Odyssey* also ends on a quiet note rather than in action or adventure. Book 23 is given over to the reunion of the long-separated husband and wife, while Book 24 features Odysseus' reunion with his father Laertes. It is true than in the final moments of the poem, a war erupts with the aggrieved families of the dead suitors, but this ending has always been suspect and has led to speculation that Homer intended something very different. In any event, by leaving some unresolved questions and not tying up all the loose ends (what will happen to Telemachos, now that his father is reinstated as king in Ithaca?), the poet, in good epic style, invites new installments in the never-ending saga.

HESIOD: THE CREATION OF PANDORA

Hesiod, who may have been a younger contemporary of Homer, composed two epics that, apart from sharing Homer's metre and diction, have little in common with the *Iliad* or *Odyssey*. In the first place, neither poem is "narrative," in the Homeric sense of having a carefully constructed plot revolving around a single unifying theme. The *Theogony* is a kind of handbook of creation, retailing all the generations of gods since the beginning of the cosmos. It consists partly of catalogs and genealogies, partly of elliptical references to many myths involving the gods that are never told in full.

The *Works and Days* is a farmer's almanac, addressed to the poet's lazy brother Perses, describing in vivid detail the rhythms of life in Hesiod's native Boeotia, in central Greece. The two poems are thus utterly different in scope and purpose, yet one brief story is equally relevant to both and is told, with minor variations, twice: the birth of Pandora.

In the *Works and Days* Pandora is recalled to explain to Perses why men's lives are a never-ending cycle of toil and hardship. It was not always so. Once men had lived free of labor and disease, but Prometheus, by stealing the fire that Zeus kept hidden from mankind, provoked the god's anger and thus inadvertently brought about far worse:

> He told glorious Hephaistos to make haste, and plaster
> earth with water, and to infuse it with a human voice
> and vigor, and make the face
>   like the immortal goddesses,
> the bewitching features of a young girl;
>   meanwhile Athene
> was to teach her her skills, and how
>   to do the intricate weaving,
> while Aphrodite was to mist her head
>   in golden endearment
> and the cruelty of desire and longings
>   that wear out the body,
> but to Hermes, the guide, the slayer of Argos,
>   he gave instructions
> to put in her the mind of a hussy,
>   and a treacherous nature.
>   So Zeus spoke. And all obeyed Lord Zeus,
>   the son of Kronos.
> The renowned strong smith modeled her figure of earth,
>   in the likeness
> of a decorous young girl, as the son of Kronos
>   had wished it.
> The goddess gray-eyed Athene dressed and arrayed her;
>   the Graces,
> who are goddesses, and hallowed Persuasion
>   put necklaces

of gold upon her body, while the Seasons,
  with glorious tresses,
put upon her head a coronal of spring flowers,
[and Pallas Athene put all decor upon her body].
But into her heart Hermes, the guide,
  the slayer of Argos,
put lies, and wheedling words
  of falsehood, and a treacherous nature,
made her as Zeus of the deep thunder wished,
  and he, the gods' herald,
put a voice inside her, and gave her
  the name of woman,
Pandora, because all the gods
  who have their homes on Olympos
had given her each a gift, to be a sorrow to men
who eat bread. Now when he had done
  with this sheer, impossible
deception, the Father sent the gods' fleet messenger,
  Hermes,
to Epimetheus, bringing her, a gift,
  nor did Epimetheus
remember to think how Prometheus had told him never
to accept a gift from Olympian Zeus,
  but always to send it
back, for fear it might prove
  to be an evil for mankind.
He took the evil, and only perceived it
  when he possessed her.

Works and Days 60–89

  The gifts of the gods were evidently contained in a great jar, and as soon as Pandora removed the lid, a mass of evils escaped to plague the human race. The notion that the agent of so much evil should be female (indeed, the first woman) was not Hesiod's invention, but was nevertheless clearly compatible with his outlook on life. He views marriage as a necessary evil and warns of the dire consequence of choosing the wrong wife (*Works and Days* 695–705; *Theogony* 603–10).

  In the *Theogony* we learn what it was that Prometheus had first done to anger Zeus. When men and gods were sharing an animal sacrifice once (in the early days, when the two races mixed freely), he tricked the king of the gods into taking for his portion the bones, concealed under a thick layer of fat, leaving for man the choice pieces of roast meat. This was Prometheus' first benefaction for mankind, before the stealing of fire, and for both he paid a heavy price. But so did man:

65

and next, for the price of the fire,
  he made an evil thing for mankind.
For the renowned smith of the strong arms
  took earth, and molded it,
through Zeus's plans, into the likeness
  of a modest young girl,
and the goddess gray-eyed Athene
  dressed her and decked her
in silverish clothing, and over her head
  she held, with her hands,
an intricately wrought veil in place,
  a wonder to look at,
and over this on her head
  she placed a wreath of gold, one
that the very renowned smith
  of the strong arms had fashioned
working it out with his hands,
  as a favor to Zeus the father.

Theogony 570–80

The account is somewhat abbreviated here, since it had already been told in the other poem, and focuses on other elements of the adornment, veil and wreath.

Greek art before the Early Classical period seems to be unaware of Pandora, or uninterested. One factor in this may be that the story has little "action" in the conventional sense in which Archaic art understood the term. Similarly, the making of Achilles' shield in *Iliad* Book 18, a great *tour de force* of poetic description, did not inspire any attempts at pictorial representation. When, in fact, scenes of Pandora do appear, in the fifth century, they mostly have that very static quality of which High Classical art was so fond.

Our earliest Pandora, on a cup of about 465 (Fig. 41), has unexpectedly been re-christened "Anesidora" ("she who releases gifts"). Hesiod had explained Pandora's name in the reverse sense, as the recipient of all the gods' gifts; but the word could also be construed to make Pandora the "giver of all gifts," and this is apparently what our painter (or his source) had in mind in renaming her. That she is still the Hesiodic Pandora is clear from the two figures surrounding her, Hephaistos and Athena. The god who fashioned her seems to be adjusting the wreath on Pandora's head, while Athena may have been busy applying jewelry. Hephaistos is shown unusually young and handsome, not at all like the Homeric image of the grizzled and unkempt smithy. Only his rear leg gives the slightest hint of his deformity. Pandora, with her arms hanging limply at her sides, looks rather lifeless – in fact quite literally so, for Athena has not yet breathed life into her.

66

Figure 41 The birth of Pandora. Attic white-ground cup, attributed to the Tarquinia Painter. London, British Museum D4. Ca. 465.

A few years later, a contemporary painter expanded the scene to fill the top frieze of a double-register calyx-krater (Figs. 42–44). Instead of following Hesiod in his choice of divinities (Horai, Charites, Peitho), he makes his own selection. Or rather, it may be that he is not illustrating the moment that interested Hesiod most, the adorning of the new creation; instead, he has imagined a later moment, when Zeus shows off his new plaything to the Olympian gods before inflicting her on mankind. Both of Zeus' messengers are present, Iris and Hermes, the latter already dashing off to earth with the news. Athena continues to work on Pandora, who once again is like a wind-up doll, still unwound. Poseidon, talking to his brother Zeus, at the left, and their sister Hera, at the right, seem only mildly curious. There is perhaps a touch of humor in the heavily armed Ares making a bee-line for Pandora. The war god always had an eye for the ladies, as we recall in the story of his flirtation with Aphrodite (*Odyssey* Book 8). The Classical period apparently found much more humor in the Pandora myth than Hesiod, for it was the subject of a satyr-play by Sophocles that may be the inspiration for the chorus of cavorting Pans in the lower frieze of this krater.

Figures 42, 43 and 44 Athena adorning Pandora in the presence of the Olympian gods. Attic red-figure calyx-krater, attributed to the Niobid Painter. London, British Museum E467. Ca. 460.

Figure 45 Epimetheus meets the newly created Pandora. Attic red-figure volute-krater, attributed to the Circle of Polygnotos. Oxford, Ashmolean Museum 525. Ca. 450.

If Hesiod had little sense of humor, he had even less sense of romance, as is evident in his sour comments on the feckless Epimetheus; but the meeting of Pandora and her future husband was an ideal image for the romanticizing tendency of Classical red-figure, as we see it on a handsome volute-krater (Fig. 45). In some respects, the scene is still further from the Hesiodic source than the previous two. Why should Pandora rise up out of the ground, as if she were Persephone returned from the Underworld? And why does Epimetheus (whose identity is assured by an inscription, as well as by the fluttering Eros symbolizing his attraction to Pandora) have the workman's clothes and mallet we would normally associate with Hephaistos? There may be some contamination from the Sophoclean satyr-play, in which a chorus of hammer-wielding satyrs tried to drive Pandora into the ground. Yet the painter has by no means forgotten his Hesiod completely. Hermes, who carries a little blossom to adorn Pandora, looks benign enough, until we recall that he was responsible for her deceptive nature, to which Epimetheus here falls victim. Pandora is, for the first time, veiled, as Hesiod says (and as is only fitting for the bride-to-be), and her elaborate diadem recalls the wrought gold that was Hephaistos' crowning touch (*Theogony* 578–84). Presiding over it all, the impresario Zeus watches calmly as his cruel plan unfolds.

In the 430s Pheidias, master-designer of the Parthenon sculptures, completed the project with the colossal gold and ivory statue of Athena for the great temple. The goddess stood on a low, wide base whose front side carried a depiction of the birth of Pandora. This information is provided by both Pausanias and Pliny the Elder, and the latter adds that twenty gods and goddesses were present – enough to fill a panel more than four metres long. The lining-up of figures on the London krater (see Figs. 42–44) is probably a not-too-distant precursor of the composition on the base, which was if anything more crowded and more static. Athena and Hephaistos, the two patrons of arts and craft, both had cult associations with the Athenian Akropolis, so it was perhaps appropriate that this consummate product of their joint handiwork, Pandora, should occupy a key location in Athena's precinct.

3

LYRIC

The term "lyric poet" encompasses a wide spectrum of men and women over many parts of the Greek world, writing in a variety of metres and genres, from as early as the seventh century until well into the fifth. Their subjects range from the highly personal (Sappho, Archilochos) to the political and topical (Alkaios, Tyrtaios, Theognis); from light verses performed at the symposium (Anakreon) to those performed at religious festivals (Alkman). Still others drew on the same body of heroic myth that Homer and other epic poets had treated, but reshaped it into shorter poems, each in his or her own distinctive voice. The vast majority of Archaic Greek lyric has come down to us in tiny fragments, either quoted out of context by late writers or on scraps of papyrus. There is almost never a connected narrative, although one papyrus of Stesichoros, made known only twenty-five years ago, comes close, and has important and interesting implications for our understanding of the visual arts.

STESICHOROS: HERAKLES AND GERYON

A native of Himera in Sicily, Stesichoros probably flourished in the early to middle years of the sixth century. He may have had a successful career as an itinerant kitharode, traveling the world and performing his own compositions to the accompaniment of the seven-stringed kithara. He drew much of his raw material from the Trojan Cycle and other epic subjects, such as the Seven against Thebes. In some instances, like his poem on the death of Agamemnon, he must have played a crucial intermediary role between the epic tradition and the dramatic reworking of Aeschylus' *Oresteia*. The assumption that Stesichoros' works were performed at festivals and other public occasions all over the Greek world, whether by him or others, would help explain their almost immediate impact on Archaic artists. In most instances, however, we have had to try to judge that impact on the basis of very scanty testimonia to the content of the poems. As a typical example, one late source claims that Stesichoros was the first poet to depict Herakles "dressed like a bandit," that is, in lion-skin, club, and bow. The implications of this for Greek art are obvious.

71

It was long known that Stesichoros wrote a lengthy poem on the story of Herakles' combat with Geryon, a triple-bodied monster who lived at the western end of the world, "beyond Ocean," and long suspected that this was the stimulus for representations of the myth in Attic vase-painting, which start about 560 and remain enormously popular for the next half-century. With the discovery of a papyrus in the sands of Egypt, we now have a few dozen verses, still only a small fraction of the original poem, but enough to give the flavor of Stesichoros as well as a number of hitherto unknown details:

> They came over the waves of the deep sea
> to the lovely island of the gods,
> where the Hesperides have their golden homes.
> (Translations of the fragments of Stesichoros are
> by the author, in some instances adapted from Page 1973)

In later tradition the stealing of the cattle of Geryon was the tenth of Herakles' twelve labors, followed by the apples of the Hesperides. This fragment also confirms that the two locations were in the same part of the world, and there seems to be a further link, in that Eurytion, Geryon's herdsman, came originally from the island of the Hesperides.

Stesichoros introduced a companion of Geryon, named Menoites, to whom he speaks before the duel with Herakles:

> The child of mighty Chrysaor and immortal
> Kallirhoë answered him and said
> "Do not try to frighten my valiant spirit with
> talk of chilling death.
> For if I am immortal by birth,
> unaging, and will have a share of life on Olympos,
> the better [to fight than be disgraced].
> But if, my friend, I am destined to endure hateful
> old age, and live among the creatures of the day,
> apart from the blessed gods,
> then it is far better that I suffer my fate."

Meanwhile, the gods on Olympos are also observing the impending combat and taking sides, a very Homeric technique. Athena, as always, protects Herakles, while Poseidon supports Geryon, who is his grandson:

> Then gray-eyed Athena said thoughtfully
> to her uncle, the stout-hearted horseman,
> "Come, remember the promise you made me,
> [not to prevent] Geryon's death."

Stesichoros' account of the climax of the struggle is, by a happy chance, preserved in the longest of the fragments:

72

[Herakles] considered alternative courses
and decided it was much better to
take on the mighty one stealthily,
and planned for him bitter destruction.
Geryon held his shield in front of him . . .
From his head the horse-plumed helmet fell to the ground . . .
The arrow with doom of hateful death about its head,
smeared with blood, agonies from the man-slaying,
speckled-necked Hydra.
In silence and stealthily it thrust into his forehead
and by divine dispensation it cleft through flesh
and bones.
And it held straight through to the top of his head
and stained with crimson blood his breastplate and
gory limbs.
And Geryon bent his head over to one side,
like a poppy that spoils its delicate shape,
shedding petals all at once.

One basic point that remains unfortunately ambiguous is just how the poet visualized Geryon. Hesiod had earlier called him "three-headed" (*Theogony* 287), but a later commentator on Hesiod adds that he had six arms, six legs, and wings. A look at the visual tradition may help to clear up the mystery.

There are a few pre-Stesichorean representations, on Corinthian vases of the seventh century, including one on which Geryon has three full bodies. The Athenian tradition also agrees on this point. A striking departure is represented by two vases probably made in a Greek colony in South Italy, very close to Stesichoros' Sicilian home, soon after the middle of the sixth century. The finer of the two has inscriptions labeling Athena, Herakles (though not Geryon), and the herdsman Eurytion, who lies dead on the ground (Figs. 46–48). Before confronting Geryon himself, Herakles has shot not only Eurytion, but also his dog Orthros, whose name is not given here but only in later sources. Geryon's wings do not occur on a single one of the Attic vases, nor does any reproduce the configuration here of three heads but only one pair of legs. The three shields and three arms wielding spears mean that he must have a total of six arms. Herakles has just released an arrow, but it does not seem to have done much harm. Behind Athena the contested cattle mill about nervously, as if aware of their master's plight. Even without the Stesichorean fragment with Athena and Poseidon, we could have assumed that the goddess protected Herakles, and would not be surprised to see her here, but it is nevertheless good to know more of her role in the poem.

In the same years that these two "Chalkidian" painters rendered Geryon with so much skill and imagination, a group of closely related painters in

Figures 46, 47 and 48 Herakles fights Geryon for his cattle as Athena looks on. Chalkidian neck-amphora. Paris, Cabinet des Médailles 202. Ca. 530.

Figure 49 Herakles fights Geryon. Attic black-figure amphora attributed to Group
E. Christchurch (New Zealand), University of Canterbury 42/57. Ca. 540.

Athens, known collectively as Group E (because they gave rise to the great
master Exekias), turned the Geryon adventure into one of their favorite
subjects. With the frequent repetition went, as so often, a certain lack of
originality, combined with these painters' characteristic taste for a rather
"stripped-down" approach to both decoration and narrative. There is, as a
rule, no Athena, no cattle, and no dog. On one example (Fig. 49), Herakles is
literally stripped down, although more often he wears his lion-skin. The
most significant feature, however, is that he fights with his club. In Attic
black-figure, his weapon is almost always the club or sword, seldom the
bow; but this is not necessarily incompatible with Stesichoros' account. We
may imagine, for example, that Herakles had first disabled Geryon by
shooting one of the three heads with an arrow and now moves against the
other two with his club. The reference to fighting "stealthily" suggests that
that first arrow was fired from some distance and caught Geryon unaware.
Eurytion clutches a wound in his thigh, presumably inflicted by the sword
slung around Herakles' chest. It is not unusual for Herakles to go into battle
with a whole arsenal of weapons. In Attic art, Geryon always has three full
bodies, joined somewhere in the middle, like Siamese twins, and one of the
painters' favorite conceits is that part of him fights on even after part has
been "fatally" wounded. The wounded body does not have very far to fall;

Figure 50 Herakles fights Geryon. Attic red-figure cup, attributed to Euphronios, side A. Munich, Antikensammlungen 2620. Ca. 510.

its head merely droops. We may see here an echo of Stesichoros' bold simile of the poppy's petals.

Geryon's burst of popularity in Attic vase-painting would not outlive the sixth century, nor would it find favor with the new red-figure style. Against all odds, Euphronios produced the most spectacular of all Geryon scenes and in many ways the one most faithful to Stesichoros (Figs. 50 and 51). One wonders if the young artist might not have heard a performance of the poem in the contests for kitharodes at the Panathenaic festival.

Spread out over both sides of an enormous cup, the scene is the first one since the Chalkidian amphora to capture some of the epic scope of Stesichoros' long (over 1500-line) poem. It captures something else too that no earlier artist had – the pathos and human drama that Stesichoros brought out, for example in Geryon's musings on his own mortality. That dimension is especially clear in the distraught woman running up behind Geryon, no doubt his mother Kallirhoë. Another fragment of the poem, too lacunose to include here, apparently had a scene between mother and son, and in fact long before Euphronios it was a favorite device of Attic painters to make heroes' mothers witness their sons' death in combat (e.g. Eos, goddess of the dawn, whose son Memnon was slain by Achilles).

Herakles wields both club and bow and arrows, to recall the several phases of the encounter. The collapsing head of Geryon has a nice Stesichorean detail, the arrow entering at about the eye and piercing straight through the head. Certain other details, such as the dog's two heads, may or

76

Figure 51 The cattle of Geryon. Side B of the cup shown in Fig. 50 (p. 76). After K. Schefold, *Götter- und Heldensagen der Griechen in der spätarchaischen Kunst* (Munich, 1978) 119, fig. 148.

may not have figured in the poem. One character who almost certainly did not is Iolaos, standing at the far left as if in conversation with Athena. This nephew and trusted companion of Herakles did accompany him on many adventures, but all our evidence, both literary and visual (apart from this vase), points to Herakles having gone alone to the far west.

The one enigma of Euphronios' great composition is the four young warriors who walk slowly behind the shuffling cattle of Geryon on the reverse (see Fig. 51). They should not be Herakles' men, since he went unaccompanied, but neither does it seem likely, as some have suggested, that this side of the cup is set at a much later moment in the myth, when Herakles was driving the cattle across Greece to his cousin Eurystheus in Tiryns. All the clues point rather to both scenes sharing the same setting: the dying Eurytion under one handle, whose body physically connects the two sides; the palm tree under the other handle, marking the location as the island of Erytheia; and one of the cattle, turning to look back in alarm. Since we have now learned of the existence of Geryon's comrade Menoites in the fragments of Stesichoros, might we imagine that he had a whole cohort of followers?

PINDAR'S VICTORY ODES

During the early years of the fifth century, the Theban poet Pindar perfected the genre known as epinician, a short (often under 100 verses) poem in honor of the victor in an athletic contest. The forty-five odes that survive mostly describe victories won between the 480s and the 450s at the four great Panhellenic Games: Olympian, Pythian (at Delphi), Nemean, and Isthmian (near Corinth). The ode might have been performed publicly, in the sanctuary where the games took place or in the home town of the victor, or privately for family and friends. Since all ethnic Greeks were eligible to compete in the games, Pindar must have traveled a great deal to take up the commissions to write and perform these odes, and in particular several of his wealthiest patrons ruled Greek cities in Sicily.

Almost every Pindaric ode has at its center a traditional myth chosen by the poet with great care to celebrate the victor and the circumstances of his victory. The myth might allow Pindar to flatter the victor by comparing him to one of the great heroes of epic, or it might evoke the heroic past of the island or city for which the victor had won glory. Or, again, the myth might embody an ethical principle that Pindar wished to present for the edification of his patron and audience. In all instances, however, the poet could count on an audience so steeped in the mythological tradition that they recognized every allusion, no matter how brief or cloaked in learned obscurity. The myth is therefore seldom narrated in a straightforward manner, but rather selectively, sometimes even polemically, when Pindar wants to dispute the version of Homer or others of his predecessors.

This elliptic handling of myth is almost antithetical to the usual approach of Greek artists, whose first priority, as we have seen, was clarity and ease of recognition. It is unlikely that Pindar ever had a strong impact on the visual arts, because of both the limited audience for his odes and his highly idiosyncratic use of myth. The odes are nevertheless a treasure-trove of stories that do not survive anywhere else in Archaic or Classical Greek literature, and yet were among the most beloved, to judge from artistic representations, by the Greeks of this period.

Olympian 1: the chariot race of Pelops and Oinomaos

The ordering of the odes in the surviving corpus is not chronological and does not follow any other obvious principle. Yet the First Olympian ode is clearly programmatic, in that its myth tells of Pelops, whose race against Oinomaos was set at Olympia and thus became an archetype for the games later held there. Pelops, from whom the Peloponnese would be named, was originally from Lydia, in Asia Minor, in the version Pindar follows. What brings him to Greece is the chance to win the hand of Hippodameia, daughter of King Oinomaos of Elis (also called Pisa), the region where Zeus' Olympian sanctuary was laid out, perhaps in the ninth century B.C. Hippodameia would be awarded to the suitor who defeated her father in a race, and many prospective husbands had forfeited their lives in the attempt. But Pelops had a most unusual chariot, one that could not fail:

But when he grew
toward the time of bloom
  and black down curled on his cheeks,
    he thought of a marriage there for his seeking –

to win from her Pisan father the girl Hippodameia.
  Going down by the dim sea,
alone in the dark, he called on the god
  of the trident, loud pounding
    Poseidon, who appeared
      and stood close by.
    "If in any way,"
  Pelops said to him,
 "the gifts of Aphrodite
count in my favor,
        shackle the bronze spear of Oinomaos,
bring me on the swiftest chariot
to Elis, and put me
within the reach
  of power, for he has slain
    thirteen suitors now, and so he delays

his daughter's marriage. Great danger
  does not come upon
the spineless man, and yet, if we must die,
why squat in the shadows, coddling a bland
old age, with no nobility, for nothing?
  As for me, I will undertake this exploit.
And you – I beseech you: let me achieve it."
He spoke, and his words found fulfillment:
  the god made him glow with gifts –
a golden chariot and winged horses never weary.

Olympian 1.67–87

Pelops could count on help from Poseidon because the god had once fallen in love with him. This typically Pindaric bit of revisionist mythmaking had been more fully explained earlier in the poem (36–51). When Tantalos was about to dismember his son Pelops and serve him up to the gods, Poseidon snatched him up to Olympos as his beloved (just like Zeus and Ganymede, as Pindar points out). The notion of gods dining on human flesh is more than Pindar can stomach.

  The ode was written in 476 for Hieron, tyrant of Syracuse, for the victory of his horse Pherenikos (named in l. 18) in the race for horse and rider. It was not the chariot race, as we might have expected, but Pindar nevertheless, toward the end of the poem, likens the divine favor enjoyed by Hieron and by Pelops. This may in part explain the absence of any reference to another version, in which Pelops won the race by a ruse: he (or Hippodameia) suborned Oinomaos' charioteer Myrtilos to fit out the car with wax linch-pins that would melt and cause the chariot to crash. Pindar's Pelops is clearly above such devious behavior. A modern jockey might object that the use of winged horses is also cheating, but Pindar's audience did not see it that way, especially when the horses were the gift of a god. What is less clear is whether Pindar rejected the story of Myrtilos or simply did not know it. Here a look at the visual tradition may offer some help.

Although the story of Pelops is attested in Archaic art only on the lost Chest of Kypselos, we do have a modest representation from the same years as Pindar's ode, on a little black-figure oil-vase (Figs. 52–54). For obvious reasons, the painters of black-figure lekythoi especially liked chariots cours-ing around the cylindrical vase. Here the painter managed to fit both teams of horses – Pelops' winged and, of course, in the lead – on the especially narrow surface. This is accomplished partly by compressing Oinomaos' horses into a kind of three-quarter view, as if they were just making a turn, while Pelops is already coming down the home stretch. Painter and poet are in complete agreement.

During the years 468–456 the great Temple of Zeus was built in the sanctuary at Olympia and one of its pediments decorated, appropriately enough, with the legend of Pelops (Fig. 55). All the principals gather as Oinomaos proclaims the race, with Zeus himself presiding, at least in spirit. Thanks to Pausanias (5.10.6), we can be certain that Myrtilos was now included. This detail, like much else about the pediments, could have been inspired by Sophocles' play *Oinomaos*, produced in 468. What the story has lost in action and vigor since Pindar, it has gained in a tension and irony that become palpable in the poses and gestures of the Olympia Master: the cocky young Pelops, swearing an oath of honor before the race and thus perjuring himself in the eyes of Zeus; the arrogant Oinomaos, announcing, unwitt-ingly, the terms of his own death; and Myrtilos (his head and knees barely visible at the left of Fig. 55), crouching quietly beside the fatal wheel, equally unaware that his treachery on behalf of Pelops will be rewarded with a treacherous murder. In its ethical implications, and in its homage to the all-powerful Zeus, the pediment does indeed have a Pindaric quality about it, even if he would have condemned its reinterpretation of the myth as "overlaid with elaboration of lies" (*Olympian* 1.29).

Yet another reinterpretation occurred in 409, when Euripides staged his own *Oinomaos*. In good Euripidean fashion, the story of the race became largely a pretext for an exploration of the power of love, both requited and unrequited, licit and illicit. Apart from the triumphant lovers Hippodameia and Pelops, Oinomaos harbors incestuous feelings for his daughter (hence the urge to kill off all the suitors), and Myrtilos is driven to treason by the promise that he will have a night with Hippodameia as his reward. It is this version that must lie behind a long series of representations in South Italian

Figures 52, 53 and *54* Chariot race of Pelops and Oinomaos. Attic black-figure lekythos attributed to the Sappho Painter. Göttingen University, J22. Ca. 500–490.

Figure 55 Preparations for the chariot race of Pelops and Oinomaos. Olympia, East Pediment, Temple of Zeus. Olympia Museum. Ca. 460.

Figure 56 Sacrifice before the chariot race of Pelops and Oinomaos. Apulian amphora attributed to the Varrese Painter. London, British Museum F331. Ca. 360–350.

vase-painting of the fourth century. Several, like an Apulian amphora (Fig. 56), focus on the preliminaries to the race. This is therefore a descendant of the Olympia pediment, but with the motif of the swearing of oaths made more explicit. Pelops wears the Oriental garb that on stage characterized his Lydian origins, while Oinomaos, a son of Ares, is in full armor. Each will pour a libation before the altar of Zeus to validate his oath. However, the erotic element is no less prominent. From the left Sterope, the queen, brings in her reluctant daughter, Hippodameia, veiled like the bride she will soon be. Does she, perhaps, catch her first glimpse of the handsome stranger at this moment? If so, he has not noticed her yet, and instead exchanges glances with Myrtilos, as the scheme hatches in his mind. Most important is the goddess Aphrodite, seated at the right as she surveys the group and gives instructions to her minion Eros. One last theatrical touch is the two heads of unsuccessful suitors, hovering in the background and even given their names.

For Pindar, the divinity who presided over the story was not Zeus, but Poseidon, whose love for Pelops brought him victory. By the late fifth century, the homoerotic motif must have seemed curiously archaic, if not outright scandalous; and for Euripides' audiences in Magna Graecia, the tempestuous passions of rich and beautiful men and women were as much an obsession as for any soap-opera addict today.

Pythian 2: Ixion on the wheel

If Pindar finds Pelops wholly admirable, he nonetheless condemns his father Tantalos, one of the four notorious sinners of Greek mythology who suffer eternal punishment in Hades (*Olympian* 1.55–60). Also among these four was Ixion, whose chilling story Pindar tells in another ode written for Hieron of Syracuse. A motif common to both Tantalos and Ixion, in which Pindar finds an important moral, is that they each enjoyed great favor from the gods, until they abused their privileged position and betrayed the trust. In Ixion's case, it was a double offense, one of passion, one of violence:

> But they say that Ixion,
> spun every way upon a winged wheel, proclaims,
> under command of the gods,
> his lesson to mankind:
> *Repay your benefactor honor's kind return!*
> And he had learned it well–
> life among the gods had been his
> to enjoy, but he could not
> enjoy it long, when he yearned
> in his frenzied thoughts
> even for Hera, the great bliss

allotted to Zeus' bed.
But Ixion's arrogance thrust him into
infatuation, and soon enough
he got what he deserved,
a unique punishment.
Two crimes brought his doom upon him.
He was the first to pollute mankind
by shedding kindred blood,
not without treachery;

and then, in the great dark inner chambers,
he reached for Zeus' wife.
But it is always necessary
to know one's limits.
Ixion's clandestine love
hurled him into disaster.
It turned upon him too,
fool, who lay with a cloud,
fondling a sweet illusion:
in shape she resembled Hera,
proudest of Uranos' children;
but it was Zeus' hand that formed
and placed her there,
a lovely affliction, to beguile him.
The four-spoked wheel

was his own doing, destruction brought on himself:
tumbling in immovable fetters, he embraced
the lesson he proclaims to all.

Pythian 2.21–41

Pindar is deliberately vague on the details of the second crime, a blood-relative treacherously murdered. Who was the victim? Later sources tell us it was his father-in-law, although strictly speaking, such a relative by marriage would not qualify as "kindred bloodshed" by the Aeschylean definition in the *Oresteia*. It is Aeschylus, a contemporary of Pindar, who first makes mention of the fact that Ixion was purified of the crime of murder by no less than Zeus (*Eumenides* 717–18). This is, of course, what made the attempted rape of Hera so much more heinous, following as it did directly on Zeus' benevolent gesture. Pindar seems to be aware of all this in the moral that he draws ("Repay your benefactor . . ."), although he suppresses any reference to the purification. Clearly the poet's main interest is in the arresting image of the wheel. Indeed, the structure of the narrative is a bit like Ixion's wheel, as it starts out with the instrument of his punishment, then, after some explanation, comes full circle, back to the image of the spinning Ixion.

Figure 57 Ixion tied to the wheel. Interior of Attic red-figure cup. Geneva, Musée d'Art et d'Histoire. Ca. 500–490.

Like Sisyphos pushing his rock, Ixion on the wheel was a distinctive visual formula, easy to draw and easy to recognize; but while Sisyphos enjoys his greatest popularity with black-figure vase-painters of the sixth century, Ixion is unknown before the beginning of the fifth.

In the years about 500 the drinking cup was coming into its own as the preferred shape of many red-figure painters, and several of them recognized at once that Ixion's wheel was predestined for a cup tondo (Fig. 57). We thus have evidence for the myth's currency in Athens a decade or two before Pindar's ode. The wheel itself is simply an enlargement of a standard chariot wheel, lacking the wings that Pindar gives it. But other elements are in complete harmony with Pindar's not too precise description. The impression that Ixion was securely and inescapably fixed to the wheel is amply borne out here, as he is attached in five places: both arms, both knees, and the neck. His running posture effectively conveys the spinning movement of the wheel, even though he is bound too tightly actually to flex his limbs. The placement of both wheel and man, slightly off the axis of the cup handles, also adds to the vertiginous effect, which was no doubt enhanced after several rounds of wine. Ixion's nudity works on two levels, both to express the humiliation of his torture and to allude to the sexual nature of his offense. Even more "Pindaric" are the overly full beard and long messy hair. These do not simply suggest that in his present predicament Ixion cannot get to a barber, but carry a much subtler iconographical message. When Ixion made his attempt on Hera, Zeus substituted for her a cloud ("Nephele" in Greek) in the likeness of his wife. The child she bore, named Kentauros, was

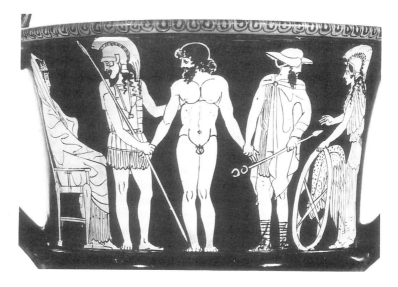

Figure 58 Ixion about to be attached to the wheel. Attic red-figure kantharos attributed to the Amphitrite Painter, side A. London, British Museum E155. Ca. 460–450.

a wild, undisciplined creature, like his father, and mated with some mares to produce the hybrid race of centaurs (*Pythian* 2.42–48). Thus Ixion's bestial, uncivilized nature, symbolized here in his unkempt appearance, was passed down through three generations.

The revolving Ixion will return to Greek art more than a century later, far from Athens. In the meantime two Athenian painters explored other aspects of the story. The earlier, about 450, clearly knew his Pindar, but either he knew other sources as well, or else he had an extraordinarily vivid imagination. In his version (Fig. 58) Ixion has not yet been fixed to the wheel, but stands exposed – literally as well as figuratively – as the perpetrator. He has been "arrested" by Hermes and an armed figure who should be Ares, and brought before his intended victim, Hera. Ixion and Ares look expectantly at her, but, seated stiffly and muffled in her cloak, she is clearly not in any mood to dispense forgiveness. Athena has brought in the wheel, now for the first time fitted with a large pair of feathery wings. When Ixion does turn to see it, he may well wonder how this curious contraption is used, for it is far too small to hold him in the usual manner. It looks more like a toy than an instrument of torture.

On the reverse of the vase (Fig. 59) the painter's power to shock and disturb is a match even for Pindar's violent language. The subject must be Ixion's earlier crime, even if the details do not reflect any known version. Ixion has just stabbed to death a young man who had sought refuge from him at an altar. The motif of murder in a sanctuary is familiar from other myths (e.g. Priam slain by Neoptolemos; cf. Figs. 116 and 117) and accords well with Pindar's emphasis on Ixion's impious nature. The victim is carefully removed by Thanatos (Death), not a threatening figure, but rather like the Thanatos who, with Hypnos (Sleep), takes Sarpedon's body from the battlefield at Troy (see Fig. 10). This beardless youth is obviously not Ixion's father-in-law, the circumstances of whose death were in any case utterly different. We simply do not know whom the painter had in mind. Ixion recoils in horror at the realization of his deed, but punishment is as swift as thought. For with the blood still fresh on the altar, a large snake has suddenly appeared, to wrap itself around Ixion and sink its teeth into his shoulder. This is the Erinys, or Fury, that torments the murderers of their own kin. A few years earlier, in 458, Aeschylus had put the Furies on stage, pursuing the matricide Orestes (cf. Figs. 102–105). Most Greek artists visualized a Fury as a winged woman wielding a snake, but this painter has reduced her to the very essence, the snake. To add to the drama, Zeus strides in from the right wielding a stone against the snake, once again a rather concrete visualization of a notion left vague in our written sources, the purification of Ixion. In its ability both to capture the dramatic climax and to merge several elements of the myth into a compact, clearly legible scene, this side of the vase recalls such Archaic models as the Boston Circe cup (see Fig. 35). By pairing this desperate frenzy with the outward calm of the other side of the vase, the artist has achieved in miniature the kind of harmonious

Figure 59 The punishment of Ixion for his first crime. Side B of the kantharos shown in Fig. 58 (p. 86).

Figure 60 Hephaistos preparing the wheel for Ixion. Fragments of Attic red-figure skyphos-krater, attributed to the Circle of the Meidias Painter. Basel, Collection of Herbert Cahn 541. Ca. 400.

balance that characterizes the two pediments of the slightly earlier Zeus Temple at Olympia (cf. Fig. 55).

One lesson the London kantharos teaches us is that those vase scenes which are the most "dramatic" are not necessarily inspired by any actual drama on the Greek stage. In the late fifth century, however, a play of Euripides on the Ixion story does seem to lie behind the last Athenian and most clearly theatrical depiction of the myth (Fig. 60). The vase was once an impressively large and fine skyphos, but only one battered portion survives. Before attaching Ixion, Hephaistos puts the finishing touches on the wheel, perhaps nailing on one of the wings. We did not know before that Hephaistos made Ixion's wheel, but that seems almost inevitable, and the vase-painters were fond of showing the smithy at work (cf. Fig. 41). His two assistants (one hand can be made out steadying the wheel) are named Kratos and Bia (Force and Violence). This pair has been borrowed, probably by Euripides, from an earlier play generally attributed to Aeschylus, in which they assisted Hephaistos in a similar task, chaining Prometheus to a rock (*Prometheus* 36–87). Behind Hephaistos, Zeus and a surprisingly maidenly Hera discuss the punishment about to be inflicted on Ixion. The criminal himself was in the lower register of figures of this big tableau, which must have been similar to the type of multi-level arrangement later so popular in Apulia. It has been conjectured that in a later scene of Euripides' play, Ixion

88

was displayed bound to the wheel, because several vases of fourth-century Magna Graecia return to the same image with which we began (see Fig. 57).

Nemean 9: the Seven against Thebes

In Pindar's often bleak vision of the world Zeus regularly metes out punishment not only to sinners like Ixion, but to the innocent and the well-intentioned too. He is not, however, a capricious or malevolent god, not like the gods of Shakespeare's cynical vision: "As flies to wanton boys, are we to th' gods, they kill us for their sport." Rather, for Pindar, men bring most of their woes on themselves, through their violent and deceitful behavior toward one another. He did not, of course, have to look very far in the corpus of Greek myth to find ample demonstration of this, but it is in his particular selection of themes and the way he shapes them that Pindar's distinctive ethical stance becomes clear. A case in point is Ajax, for whom Pindar has tremendous sympathy because he was cheated of the arms of Achilles that he rightly deserved, by the cleverness of Odysseus and the indifference of the Greek army (Nemean 7 and 8). Another instance is the story of the Seven against Thebes, which shows man's nature at its best and its worst, with the latter more often prevailing.

The story of the fratricidal power-struggle between Eteokles and Polyneikes was told in epic and later dramatized (e.g. Aeschylus' Seven against Thebes), but Pindar begins his account with an earlier, not dissimilar struggle. Adrastos and Amphiaraos were rivals for power in Argos, until Adrastos was driven out, eventually becoming king of nearby Sikyon. Later the two were reconciled, Amphiaraos marrying Adrastos' sister Eriphyle and promising to abide by her decision in any future disagreement. When Adrastos later organized the attack on Thebes, on behalf of his son-in-law Polyneikes, Amphiaraos was compelled to join the ill-fated expedition. Pindar summarizes the whole cycle in a highly abbreviated fashion:

> He had come there fleeing dread Amphiaraos
> and the deadly strife at home in Argos.
> For the sons of Talaos, crushed in that struggle,
> were princes no more. The man of greater might
> puts an end to the order of old.
> But the sons of Talaos betrothing
> Eriphyle the man-subduer
> as a pledge of trust to Oïkles' son,
> once more were mightiest of the fair-haired Danaans,
> and in time they led a host of men
> to seven-gated Thebes.
> No propitious omens sent them on their way,
> nor did Kronos' son,

hurling the lightning bolt,
bid them, in their madness, to set forth from home –
rather to refrain from going.

But they were massed together,
hastening to sure disaster
with brazen arms and caparisoned steeds:
yielding up all hope of a sweet return,
they fattened the white bloom of smoke
with their corpses;
by the banks of Ismenos,
seven pyres fed on their youthful flesh.
But with all-powerful thunder
Zeus cleft the deep-breasted earth for Amphiaraos
and hid him from sight, chariot and all.

Nemean 9.13–25

Eriphyle is described, with sinister overtones, as the "pledge of trust" of the oath between Adrastos and Amphiaraos and as the "man-subduing" woman. Here Pindar alludes obliquely to a part of the story he chooses not to tell, how Eriphyle, bribed with a necklace by Polyneikes, forced her husband to go to his death. Amphiaraos is thus, at different times, both aggressor and victim, his death made more poignant by the fact that, as a seer, he knows it is coming but, bound by his oath, is helpless to avoid it. Yet even in death Amphiaraos will exact a terrible revenge on Eriphyle, for their son, only a small boy at the time of the march of the Seven, would later murder his mother, much like Orestes and Klytaimestra.

The lost epic *Thebaid* must have included a vivid description of Amphiaraos departing for Thebes, because this is the moment preferred by most Archaic vase-painters. Only in the fifth century do they start to fill in other aspects of the cycle, although it was never treated as fully as, say, the Trojan Cycle. A red-figure painter working just a few years after the date of Pindar's ode (472) produced what is perhaps our only depiction of the reconciliation of Adrastos and Amphiaraos (Fig. 61). The schema of the two warriors going at each other with drawn swords, with comrades trying to hold them back, is a popular one in Attic vase-painting and often refers to the struggle over the arms of Achilles (cf. Fig. 109). However, the woman intervening so conspicuously tells us we are not at Troy, but in some other myth, and Sir John Beazley saw that she must be Eriphyle. Thus the sequence of events that Pindar imagines stretching over years – Adrastos driven out and later negotiating Eriphyle's marriage to Amphiaraos – is here compressed into an instant, making use of a well established iconographical formula.

Whereas the sixth century had focused almost exclusively on Amphiaraos and the heavy irony of his reluctant departure from Argos, red-figure of the

90

early fifth preferred to show the gathering of all the Seven, among whom Amphiaraos and Adrastos are not always easy to pick out. Only one particularly ambitious painter combined elements of the Archaic tradition with the more recent, as well as some original to him, to create his own Theban Cycle (Figs. 62 and 63). The preparations for departure of the Seven are spread over both sides of the exterior, with a four-horse chariot forming the focal point of each side. Beside one of these chariots stands a woman holding a small boy on her arm – Eriphyle and Alkmeon – as Amphiaraos mounts the car. Modestly veiled, Eriphyle looks like the model wife, although the sword that she hands her husband hints darkly at her treachery. A balding old man belongs to this family group as well, perhaps Amphiaraos' father. The chariot on the other side should then belong to Adrastos, although the painter has not favored us with any inscriptions. With the help of a similar scene that carries a single inscription, we can recognize as Parthenopaios, who in one tradition was a brother of Adrastos, the bearded warrior cutting off a lock of hair with his sword. The inside of the cup (see Fig. 63) gives us the sequel, or at least the one moment from the battle for Thebes that sums up most perfectly its futility and horror: Eteokles and Polyneikes, brothers and rivals, plunge their swords into each other at the same instant.

The actual clash of the two armies is an extremely rare subject, for several reasons. The Greeks, both in their poetry and their art, were far more

Figure 61 Eriphyle resolving the dispute between Adrastos and Amphiaraos. Attic red-figure column-krater attributed to the Kaineus Painter. Naples, Museo di Capodimonte 958. Ca. 460. After *LIMC* I pl. 567.

Figure 62 Preparation of the Seven against Thebes. Fragments of Attic red-figure cup, attributed to the Kleophrades Painter, exterior. Athens, National Museum, Akropolis 336. Ca. 500–490.

Figure 63 Eteokles and Polyneikes killing one another. Interior of the cup shown in Fig. 62 (above). After B. Graef and E. Langlotz, *Die antiken Vasen von der Akropolis zu Athen* II (Berlin, 1933) pl. 25.

Figure 64 The Seven against Thebes. Attic red-figure volute-krater attributed to the Painter of Bologna 279. Ferrara, Museo Nazionale 3031 (T579). Ca. 450. After K. Schefold, *Die Sagen von den Argonauten, von Theben und Troia in der klassischen und hellenistischen Kunst* (Munich, 1989) 79, fig. 60.

interested in the exploits of individual heroes than of whole armies. We have noticed how Homer, although he may occasionally refer to the vastness of the forces on both sides, always quickly focuses in on the single combat of particular heroes. Similarly, although hundreds of warriors are named in the *Iliad* once – usually at the moment they are killed – a tiny handful recur over and over, standing out from the crowd, and gradually taking on clearly defined and subtly differentiated personalities. The visual arts follow suit, much preferring a duel or other heroic deed to a great panorama of war. One of the brief periods when a few artists did experiment with this latter genre was in the years about the middle of the fifth century, under the influence of mural painters who created such expansive compositions to fill the walls of shrines, stoas, and other public buildings. An impressive example is a big volute-krater in Ferrara, the shape perhaps best suited to this grandiose style (Fig. 64). Since there are no inscriptions and the warriors do not seem to be armed or dressed (or undressed) in iconographically significant ways, we would be hard pressed to decide which epic battle is meant, were it not for one vivid detail immediately recognizable from Pindar. At the bottom of the scene, a warrior and his younger companion are slipping into the ground, the warrior signaling his distress with a raised hand. The four horses of his team flounder about as they too are swallowed up by the earth. It is, of course, Amphiaraos, suffering the most exquisite punishment that Zeus reserved for him.

The first impression of utter chaos is belied, on closer examination, by the neat symmetry and careful articulation of the scene. It is a quintessentially "Homeric" battle, composed of a series of duels between heroes so evenly matched that there is no hint of the outcome. The only exception to the pattern is at the lower right, where a third warrior collapses between the duelling pair. Assuming that he was meant to be Amphiaraos' opponent, we have exactly seven pairs of fighters; but too much symmetry quickly loses its appeal, and the painter has slipped in one enigmatic element. An unarmed man in traveling clothes seems to have wandered in from the right and observes the mêlée with an oddly calm detachment. Occupying a plane that is neither the upper nor the lower, overlapping one warrior and overlapped by another, he enhances the sense of three-dimensional space, yet is not physically part of it. One intriguing suggestion calls him Oedipus, whose self-imposed exile from Thebes led ultimately to the sorry state of civil war that culminates here.

Pythian 4: Jason and the Argonauts

Pindar's very sketchy resumé of the Seven against Thebes makes us realize how little we know of the Theban Cycle, which must once have rivaled the tale of Troy in the popular imagination. In one respect, indeed, the Theban was even richer than the Trojan Cycle, for it was a multi-generational saga, encompassing such diverse heroes as Kadmos, Pentheus, Oedipus, and their respective families. Yet another of the great cornerstones of Archaic epic that is now lost to us is the story of Jason and his quest for the golden fleece, or *Argonautika*, after the ship Argo in which they sailed. Whereas the loss of the epic *Thebaid* is partly compensated for by Attic tragedy's intense interest in the Theban Cycle (see Chapter 4, on Euripides' *Bacchae*), the *Argonautika* did not lend itself so well to dramatization, apart from its sequel, made famous by Euripides, the story of Medea and Jason in Corinth (see Chapter 4, on *Medea*). Nevertheless, in the Early Hellenistic period (ca. 275 B.C.) Apollonios of Rhodes tried to resurrect the genre of Archaic epic with a long hexameter poem on the Argonauts. Thanks to the poet's antiquarian interests and enormous learning, his epic is a gold-mine for the modern mythographer; but to find an earlier account of Jason and the Argonauts we must turn to Pindar, who lavished greater attention on this myth than any other.

Pythian 4, more than double the length of any of Pindar's other odes, honors the royal family of Cyrene (in modern-day Libya), tracing its origins back to one Euphamos, who took part in the voyage of the Argo. This slender thread is enough for Pindar to hang an unusually detailed account of Jason, beginning with a rather Homeric-style catalog of the heroes who answered the call from all over Greece and made up the Argo's crew. The narrative continues at an uncharacteristically leisurely pace, as the Argo

makes its way to the far shores of the Black Sea, to Colchis, home of King
Aeetes and his daughter Medea. Here the story accelerates with their arrival:
Medea's love for Jason (later described by Apollonios in excruciating detail)
and the magic protective ointment she supplies are briskly recounted. Before
Jason can claim the fleece – no easy task itself, since it is guarded by a fierce
serpent-dragon – he must pass a test imposed by Aeetes, to yoke a pair of
fire-breathing bulls and plow the king's field:

> But now Aietas threw down before him
> the adamantine plow, and brought out bulls
> snorting streams of blazing fire through their jaws,
> pawing the earth with brazen hooves.
> > > > > > Single-handed,
> he led them to the yoke, tied them in, and drove them
> plowing the furrows straight, digging a fathom deep
> into the earth's brown back.
> > > > > And then he spoke:
> "Let the ship's master try his hand at this,
> this first: and then the imperishable coverlet,
> the fleece fringed with gleaming gold."
> So Aietas cast the challenge,
> and Jason took it up.
> > > > > Trusting in the gods,
> he let his purple cloak drop to the ground.
> > Medea's skill in potions
> > > kept the fire from his flesh;
> > > > he gripped the plow,
> > > bound the bulls' necks to the yoke,
> > and, stabbing their stout-ribbed flanks
> with a pointed goad,
> > > > > > he toiled through
> his allotted measure.
> > Aietas, astonished at his power,
> > > uttered a wordless cry.
>
> But his comrades stretched their hands
> toward the man in triumph, raining
> bayleaf garlands
> > > > > and warm shouts upon him.
> But grimly the son of Helios pointed the way
> > to the shimmering fleece,
> > > where Phrixos with his blade
> > > > had flayed the ram and spread it out.
> > He had no inkling yet
> > that Jason would succeed,

for the fleece lay in a thicket,
                                    and a dragon
loomed above it, foam
    dripping from its cruel jaws, huger
        than a fifty-oared, iron-bolted ship.

But it's a long way by the main road,
                                    and time presses.
I know a certain shortcut, for I am guide to many
in the turns of song.
                        Arkesilas, Medea's wiles
helped him past that green-eyed, speckle-backed serpent;
and she took part in her own abduction, she, Pelias' ruin.
                                    Pythian 4.224–50

The climactic moment, the taking of the fleece, is curiously truncated, with the poet's disingenuous excuse that he has gone on too long already and must bring the poem rapidly to a close. Not that he, in fact, does this, although he does return quickly to the victor's family, via the Argonauts' brief stop on Lemnos, where their ancestor Euphamos founded the line. Nor does Pindar show any interest in Jason's return to Greece or Medea's later career, save for those last, ominous words, "Pelias' ruin." His listeners, of course, recognized the story of how Medea, once back in Thessaly with Jason, duped the daughters of old Pelias into killing and dismembering their father with a promise of rejuvenating him. For this reason Jason and Medea had to flee his homeland, settling in Corinth, where Euripides would take up their story.

The *Argonautika* never rivaled the popularity of other epic cycles in any period of Greek art. Archaic vase-painting tended to prefer those episodes that are peripheral to Jason and his quest for the fleece, such as the just-mentioned story of Medea and the daughters of Pelias or the lavish funeral games later held for this same Pelias, the usurper who sent Jason out in search of the fleece. Pindar was not the first to stress the role of Aphrodite in the story of Jason, for a century earlier, on the Chest of Kypselos, was a scene of Medea enthroned between Aphrodite and Jason, with the caption, "Aphrodite commands: Jason marries Medea." In extant art, however, it is not easy to find a single depiction of Jason before the fifth century, let alone the fleece.

In Classical art, by contrast, Jason is a familiar figure, and there is a tremendous interest in the fleece, both on and off the hoof. For the origin of this fleece, entirely ignored by Pindar, was the golden ram that rescued Phrixos and his sister Helle from their wicked stepmother Ino and brought Phrixos (Helle having fallen off, into the body of water that bears her name, the Hellespont) safely to Colchis. Both Attic red-figure and South Italian depicted Phrixos clinging to the ram, and Apollonios adds the touching

Figure 65 Jason taking the Golden Fleece. Attic red-figure column-krater attributed to the Orchard Painter. New York, Metropolitan Museum 1934.11.7. Ca. 470–460.

detail that the ram itself spoke to Phrixos and instructed him to sacrifice it to Zeus and remove the fleece (*Argonautika* 1.673–64).

The taking of the fleece is, as we would expect, the moment preferred by most artists. Pindar offered them nothing to go on here, and the variations they introduced are remarkable. An Athenian contemporary of Pindar gives us our earliest representation (Fig. 65). The fleece hangs on a rock, an alternative to the tree that will later become standard. The snake has wound itself several times around this boulder, giving it a tremendous length but hardly the girth that Pindar would have us believe; but then Jason is strangely emaciated as well, leading some commentators to wonder if the scene was meant to be taken altogether seriously. Yet nothing else about it suggests a parody, and Jason's unheroic proportions might suggest a motif that Apollonios would later exploit much more fully: Jason's success is utterly dependent on the females, both human and divine, around him. Here great prominence is given to Athena, dominating the scene and gently urging Jason on. This is not the first time we have observed this quirk of Athenian vase-painters, inserting their city goddess in places where she does not belong, making her the universal protectress of heroes (see e.g. Figs. 33, 50), nor will it be the last (cf. Figs. 73, 75). At the right, the stern of the Argo appears, decorated with a woman's head in good nautical tradition. Since all sources agree that the fleece was concealed deep in a wood, we should not imagine that our painter has moved it to the seashore. Rather, he wants only to remind us that the ship herself is one of the protagonists of the myth, built

Figure 66 Jason takes the Golden Fleece. Italiote red-figure volute-krater, attributed to the Sisyphos Painter, lower frieze. Munich, Antikensammlungen 3268. Ca. 420.

under the watchful eye of Athena. The bearded man who turns to watch must be Aeetes, looking as little like a villain as Jason looks like a hero. The painter has lavished most of his care on Athena.

When we leave Athens for Magna Graecia, Athena, not surprisingly, disappears from the scene (Fig. 66). Her place is promptly taken by Medea, who displays the box of pharmaka (potions, poisons, and the like) that is often her attribute in Greek art. Jason now looks considerably more heroic, as he moves purposefully with drawn sword. In fact his pose is modeled on that favorite real-life Athenian, Aristogeiton, who (with his friend Harmodios) murdered the tyrant Hipparchos in 514 B.C. and was honored with a public statue in just this pose. Even Jason's garment, the chlamys pinned at the right shoulder and unfurling as a shield, copies the sculptural prototype.

This three-figure group – Medea, Jason, snake – makes a pleasing composition that would be suitable, say, for a carved marble relief; but the painter had to fill a long frieze, which he did, logically enough, with a gathering of the crew of the Argo. Among these rather similar young men, we can pick out two with wings, the sons of the North wind, Boreas. Archaic art was fond of these twins, especially their moment of glory on the outward journey, when they used their flying ability to rout the Harpies that had fouled the food of the blind seer Phineus. The frieze on our vase is very much in the late-fifth-century style that the first generation of Athenian vase-painters brought with them to South Italy. It is a style unfortunately characterized by exceedingly languid young men (and women), who here look rather bored with the life-and-death struggle of their captain.

Nemean 3: Chiron and Achilles

Earlier in *Pythian* 4, Pindar had told the famous story of how Jason first came to Iolkos, the land of his forefathers, to claim the throne from which his father had been deposed by the usurper Pelias. He was recognized by the single sandal that he wore (the other lost in the mud), the fulfillment of a prophecy. But when asked his identity, he responds not, as expected, with his parentage, but with a proud description of his upbringing in a rather unorthodox family:

> And Jason, unintimidated, answered him
> in gentle words: "This I have to say,
> that I will show
>   my upbringing by Chiron.
> Yes, I come from Chariklo and Philyra,
>   from the cavern
>   where Centaur's daughters reared me:
>   for twenty years I lived with them,
>   not once, in word or deed,
>   bringing them shame."
>
> *Pythian* 4.102–6

Remembering Pindar's earlier reference to the barbarous race of centaurs, offspring of the wicked Ixion, we may be surprised that one particular centaur, Chiron, was not only famed for his wisdom, but presided over an exemplary family comprising three generations of devoted females. Even greater than Jason was Chiron's other pupil, Achilles, whose education was a favorite subject for both poets and artists in Greece and Rome.

If Achilles appears often in the pages of Pindar, it is not only because of his privileged position as the greatest of the Homeric heroes, but also for a more topical reason. Many of the victors Pindar celebrates came from the island of Aegina, a neighbor (and often enemy) of Athens. Aegina claimed as its heroic ancestors Aiakos, his sons, Peleus and Telamon, and their sons, Achilles and Ajax, respectively. By the second generation the family had left Aegina, Peleus for Thessaly and Telamon for the nearby island of Salamis, but for Pindar's purposes this made Achilles and Ajax no less Aeginetan. Ajax's tragic end is always, as we have noted, treated with great compassion by Pindar, and Achilles was the perfect hero to whom an athletic victor could be likened.

Not only did Achilles have the noble ancestry that Pindar values so highly, but also the finest education and preparation for manhood, thanks to his famous teacher:

> Blond Achilleus, while still a child
>   at play about Philyra's house, performed
>   deeds of might: often brandishing

99

his iron javelin, swift as the wind,
he battled savage lions
                              to their deaths
and slew boars, dragging
    their bodies, trembling
        in the last gasp,
                          to Chiron the centaur;
this from the time he was six and ever after.
    Artemis was amazed
and bold Athena marveled to see him

killing stags without the help of hounds
    or traps: he ran them down
        on foot. And men of old tell how
    shrewd Chiron raised Jason also,
in his house of stone,
                          and reared Asklepios,
whom he taught the mild-handed use
    of salves and drugs.
        And it was Chiron
                          who saw to the wedding
of Nereus' radiant daughter and brought up
    her dread child Achilleus,
raising his thoughts in all things noble.
                          Nemean 3.43–58

From this we learn what was considered the best training for a future hero, namely hunting, because this developed the skills he would need most on the battlefield: speed in running and accuracy with a spear. It is no accident that the little Achilles, who could outrun a deer, grew up to be the "swift-footed" hero of the *Iliad*. It is also no coincidence that the best teacher of hunting is the centaur, himself a forest-dweller who lived from hunting and would know intimately the haunts and habits of all species of wild animal.

Chiron, however, is versed in more than hunting, even the most refined art of medicine, which he taught to Asklepios and, by some accounts, to Achilles as well. He is also talented as a matchmaker, in particular between Achilles' parents, Peleus and the sea-nymph Thetis, daughter of Nereus. Chiron married these two, as Pindar says here, but even before that he saw to it that this somewhat unlikely couple – a mortal man and a goddess – got together, as Zeus himself decreed. Peleus nearly fell victim to a plot of his enemy Akastos, but Chiron intervened:

but Chiron prevented it,
and the destiny decreed of Zeus
came to fulfillment:
Peleus, having withstood the blaze

of all-consuming fire,
the keen claws and dread fangs of ravening lions,

married one of the Nereids on high.
Nemean 4.60–65

Although the events of the story are scattered over several odes, a picture gradually emerges of Chiron as a kind of benevolent godfather, watching over Achilles' whole family, first his parents and then the young hero himself. The visual tradition likewise accorded Chiron an honored place in the saga of Achilles, from as early as the seventh century. Each stage of the story – the courtship of Peleus and Thetis, their wedding, and the education of Achilles – is well represented, each reaching its peak of popularity at a different period.

The courtship was a particular favorite of Athenian red-figure painters of the fifth century. Chiron is present on a number of these versions, such as one of the latest, a hydria of about 440 (Fig. 67). Peleus reaches for Thetis, who daintily tries to avoid his grasp, as one of her sister Nereids echoes the same gestures. Thetis' ability to metamorphose herself into various creatures and even inanimate substances (fire) fascinated both Pindar and Archaic painters, but by the High Classical period of this vase may have seemed quaintly old-fashioned. The portrayal of Peleus as a young hunter, complete with conical cap, laced boots, spears and hunting-dog, recalls the emphasis placed by the myth on the hunting skills of both Chiron and Achilles. The

Figure 67 Peleus wrestles with Thetis as Chiron observes. Attic red-figure kalpis in the manner of Polygnotos. Formerly Swiss Market. Ca. 440. After X. Krieger, *Der Kampf zwischen Peleus und Thetis in der griechischen Vasenmalerei* (Münster, 1975) pl. 7,1.

101

centaur himself calmly oversees the chase from the left, satisfied that all is going according to plan. His human head, with its full beard and slightly unkempt hair, could be that of a Classical philosopher, were it not for the pointed animal's ear.

The reason Thetis had to be married off to a mortal man was that it had been foretold that she would give birth to a son greater than his father. With that, Zeus and Poseidon, who had earlier fancied her, immediately lost interest, but compensated Thetis for the indignity of marrying beneath her by staging one of the great weddings of Greek myth, with all the gods invited. The wedding also had a darker side, for it was here that the chain of events that would lead to the Trojan War had its origin; but for Early Archaic artists it was primarily an excuse for a dazzling assemblage of gods in a festive atmosphere. Kleitias, for example, on the François Vase, shows the guests moving slowly toward the home of Peleus, who greets Chiron, the first to arrive, with a handshake (see Fig. 20). The first arrivals are on foot, while the rest approach both in chariots and on foot (see Fig. 19). Chiron has brought a whole assortment of freshly killed animals for the wedding feast, suspended from a long branch that he often carries. The roast meat will be washed down with the wine that Dionysos carries in a heavy amphora on his shoulder. We can imagine Chiron years later happily filling that pole with the animals Achilles has hunted down and brought home. Among the ladies coming up just behind Chiron is Chariklo, his wife. The bride herself is only glimpsed through the open door of her new home.

A century later a red-figure artist re-imagined almost the very same moment, in a manner more in keeping with both Classical Athenian weddings and Pindar's perception of Chiron (Figs. 68 and 69). Once again the procession approaches the house, in which we see the bedchamber all decked out for the newly-weds. Now, however, the parental role has been entirely taken over by Chiron and his mother Philyra. The latter stands before the house, and both she and her son hold torches to light the way, since weddings regularly took place at night. This is the only inscribed representation of Chiron's mother, but the painter must have been well aware that, as Pindar puts it, Chiron lived "in the house of Philyra." Peleus, leading his modest bride by the hand, presents her to Chiron as if to his own father. We now understand it was inevitable that Achilles would later be raised by Chiron and Philyra, after his natural mother abandoned him to return to her watery home. The remainder of the procession retains only a little of the splendor of the earlier scene, particularly in the figure of Apollo lending the music of his kithara to the joyous occasion. Interestingly, the notion that weddings are quintessentially family affairs, for both host and guests, that was so apparent on the François Vase, is equally clear here: Apollo is surrounded by his sister Artemis (also holding torches) and mother Leto, while at the back of the procession comes Dionysos with *his* mother Semele.

The subject of Peleus entrusting his young son to the centaur Chiron has

Figures 68 and 69 The wedding of Peleus and Thetis. Attic red-figure neck-amphora, attributed to the Copenhagen Painter. New York, Collection of Shelby White and Leon Levy. Ca. 470.

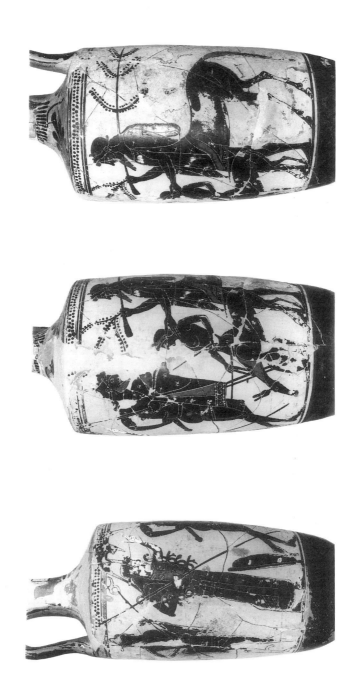

Figures 70, 71 and 72 Peleus visiting Chiron and Achilles. Attic black-figure lekythos attributed to the Edinburgh Painter. Athens, National Museum 550. Ca. 500–490.

its place in Attic art between the two chronological extremes we have just considered, and especially on black-figure vases of the late sixth century. Achilles may be anything from a babe in arms to a well developed adolescent. On one example of about 500, he is meant to be roughly the 6-year-old that Pindar describes (Figs. 70–72). If his anatomy looks too developed for the age of 6, this is due to the inability of Archaic artists to portray children as anything other than miniature adults; but then again, what 6-year-old performs the feats ascribed to this *wunderkind*? This is not, strictly speaking, Achilles being turned over to Chiron, which happened soon after his birth. We must rather imagine that Peleus made regular visits to Chiron's mountain home, to check on his son's progress. On this occasion, Achilles has been practising the spear throw, in which Pindar tells us he excelled. The gentle deer beside him suggests that, in his time in the wild, Achilles has come to know the animals not simply as hunted prey, but as intimate companions. Pose and gesture are particularly effective in conveying the text of this friendly encounter: Peleus casually scrutinizing his young son; Chiron proudly showing off his protégé; and Achilles dutifully greeting his father but eager to resume his exercises. To complete the circle of the lekythos, the painter has added Athena and Hermes, the former cheerfully waving to Chiron. We have often noticed how Athena will join any hero, at any time, just to show her friendly interest. Here it seems appropriate that she displays her armor so conspicuously, as if to show the young Achilles what he has to look forward to.

Nemean 1: the infant Herakles

If Achilles was hunting wild beasts at the tender age of 6, he was nevertheless a latecomer to heroic struggles in comparison with Herakles, who had his first brush with death while still in swaddling clothes. Given Pindar's interest in the early lives of the heroes, along with his propensity to reach for the less familiar Herakles myths, it is perhaps no surprise that he gives us our fullest account of Herakles' first heroic feat, and indeed the only literary account of Archaic or Classical date. Unlike most of Pindar's myths, the story has no particular moral or association with the victor (a Syracusan), but is told for the sheer joy in this miraculous tale, with a dash of unaccustomed humor.

Pindar passes over the well known circumstances of Herakles' conception and birth, only briefly hinting that it was not an easy delivery for Alcmena, who carried twins by different fathers: Herakles, son of Zeus, and Iphikles, son of her mortal husband Amphitryon:

> But when I move among the heights
> of triumph, Herakles comes to mind. I embrace him
> eagerly, stirring to life again the ancient story,

how that child of Zeus,
                       having survived
the throes of birth and come with his twin brother
from his mother's womb into the sudden wondrous light,
did not escape the notice of Hera
    when he was laid
        in purple swaddling bands.
           Stung to the heart with wrath,
        the Queen of the gods
dispatched a pair of serpents.
                           Through the open doors
into the wide inner chambers they glided,
        to wind themselves around the babes,
           eager to snatch them in their jaws.
But Herakles raised his head
                  and made first trial of battle,
gripping both snakes by their throats,
    one in each unshakable hand.
        Moment by moment,
           strangling,
        the life-breath
fled their hideous coils.
                    Unbearable terror struck
the women in attendance on Alkmena.
        She herself, leaping to her feet
           just as she was, in her bed-clothes,
had tried
        to keep the monsters at bay.

And the chiefs of the Kadmeians arrived together
in haste, with a rattle of bronze arms,
Amphitryon among them, sword in hand,
shaken with anxiety.
                For every man feels the weight
of sorrows at home, while troubles elsewhere
do not hold the heart for long.
He stood there, wavering
    between terror and delight,
        for he could see the unearthly
           strength and power of this son.

Nemean 1.33–58

Amphitryon's delight in his son's prowess is tempered by the sudden realization that this son is not his. Zeus had shared his wife's bed for a night, although she had no idea at the time. Pindar quickly turns serious again, bringing on the Theban seer Teiresias, to prophesy Herakles' later career, right up to his apotheosis and marriage on Olympos to Hebe, the final reconciliation with his new mother-in-law Hera.

Pindar certainly did not invent this story, for a few years earlier than his ode a red-figure painter produced a sophisticated and self-assured rendering of it (Fig. 73). The scene could almost be read as an illustration of Pindar, if it were not slightly earlier and did not include Athena, the ubiquitous protectress of heroes. The boys are indeed twins, except that Herakles has blond hair, a trait that, because of its rarity in Greece, seems to be reserved for special people (we recall Achilles' blond hair at *Nemean* 3.43). Although Herakles has a good grip on each snake, they look far from dead, hence Alcmena's fright as she snatches up the helpless Iphikles is quite legitimate. Pindar implies that it was her servant-girls who first noticed the commotion in the babies' room, and here one of them watches from the left. Understandably, the painter was not about to bring the Theban army into this little bedchamber and instead puts Amphitryon in civilian clothes, as though he has come with his wife from their own bedroom nearby.

The reverse of this vase presents an enigmatic scene that may or may not have some thematic connection to the front (Fig. 74). Zeus, holding his scepter in one hand and thunderbolt in the other, dispatches his two messengers, Hermes and Iris, who race off in opposite directions. The centripetal composition does not have the feel of a complete, self-contained scene, but rather an excerpt from something larger. Where are the divine messengers going, and what is Zeus' intent? It would surely be an overly subtle interpretation to see here a visualization of the "contradictory message" sent by the immortals to Amphitryon; but in light of the great care with which the vase has been designed and executed, it may be legitimate to see a more general thematic link. Zeus has just been revealed as the father of one of these boys; his daughter Athena is already there to attest to it. Now he sends out his messengers to proclaim the identity of his hero son and perhaps to placate the dubious father and bewildered mother. Whatever discomfort they feel at Zeus' deception will be more than compensated by the glory of being mother and stepfather to the greatest of all Greek heroes.

Some two generations later, another red-figure painter took up the subject of the infant Herakles (Fig. 75). In one respect only is the scene even closer to Pindar: Amphitryon arrives with drawn sword. Otherwise, most differences from the earlier vase are best explained by artistic developments of the intervening forty years. So, for example, the boys are now more convincingly childlike, although still not exactly babies. Certainly babies do not make the kind of supplicating gesture with which Iphikles turns to his frightened mother for help. The whole composition is streamlined, in the Classical manner, by eliminating the extra onlooker. Finally, Athena has taken up a position in the very center and does not so much participate in the scene as preside over it. In this sense, she recalls the Athena put by the same

Figure 73 Baby Herakles strangling snakes. Attic red-figure stamnos, attributed to the Berlin Painter, side A. Paris, Louvre G192. Ca. 480.

Figure 74 Zeus sends out Hermes and Iris. Side B of the stamnos shown in Fig. 73 (above).

108

Figure 75 Baby Herakles strangling snakes. Attic red-figure hydria, attributed to the Nausikaa Painter. New York, Metropolitan Museum 25.28. Ca. 440.

painter into his version of the meeting of Odysseus and Nausikaa (see Fig. 28). With her gleaming helmet and raised arm leaning on her spear, she may well be a miniature copy of a great bronze statue of the goddess that was one of the landmarks of the Athenian Akropolis in the time of Perikles.

BACCHYLIDES: DITHYRAMBS

A slightly younger contemporary of Pindar, Bacchylides was a native of the small island of Keos, near Athens, made famous in literary circles by his uncle Simonides. In the 470s and 460s Pindar and Bacchylides seem to have been on the same "circuit," occasionally writing victory odes for the same patrons, especially in Sicily. Bacchylides' victory odes have often suffered by comparison with Pindar's, but he also wrote poetry in other genres that has its own particular genius. For example, two poems are preserved that were composed for performance at religious festivals, one in Athens, the other on the sacred island of Delos. Both belong to the genre known as the dithyramb, a forerunner of Attic tragedy, and both celebrate Athens' national hero, Theseus.

Bacchylides 18: Theseus' youthful deeds

Although he was to become the pre-eminent heroic symbol of Athens, Theseus was, ironically, not an Athenian by birth. His mother Aithra was

109

the daughter of the king of Troizen, at the north-east corner of the Peloponnese, and he was conceived during a brief sojourn there of the Athenian king Aegeus. To protect Aithra's honor, the story was given out that the god Poseidon was the child's true father, a story which, as we shall see, will have important implications for Theseus' later career. Aegeus left behind in Troizen a sword and a pair of sandals concealed under a heavy rock, the tokens by which he would later recognize his only son. The adolescent Theseus, as soon as he could lift the rock, set out for Athens to claim his true patrimony. Although his mother and grandfather begged him to travel by sea, he preferred the more dangerous land route, around the Saronic gulf, that was infested with brigands and bandits. These would be the first test of his heroic mettle.

Bacchylides' poem is a "lyric dialogue in dramatic form" (Neils 1987: 8) between Aegeus and a chorus of Athenians, as Theseus approaches the city of Athens to great wonder and amazement:

> Just now a herald came on foot
>   from the tortuous Isthmian path
> to tell of unspeakable deeds done
>   by a prodigious man. Mighty Sinis
> he killed – strongest of men
>   he was, grandson of Cronus and son
>   of the Lytaean earthquake-maker!
> This man has slain the murderous
> sow of the meadow of Cremmyon;
>   has killed dread Sciron as well;
> has captured the wrestling school
>   that Cercyon ran, while Procoptes
> has dropped the hideous mattock
>   Polyphemus made, faced with one
> stronger than he! The end of these deeds I fear.
>
> Two [men], he says, accompany the unknown one.
>   Down from his gleaming shoulder
> hangs a sword with an ivory hilt,
>   polished javelins in his hands,
> and a Spartan dogskin cap
>   covers his ruddy curls.
>   A purple shirt is wrapped
> round his body and over that
> a woolen mantle from Thessaly; from his eyes
>   a spark of Lemnian fire
> flashes red. He is a boy
>   scarce grown, eager for games
> of Ares, wanting war

110

and the battle clash of bronze. He comes
seeking Athens where splendor is.
Bacchylides 18.16–30; 46–60

These are the portions of the poem spoken by King Aegeus. Five opponents
of Theseus are named, four human (Sinis, Skiron, Kerkyon, and Prokrustes,
here called "Procoptes") and one beast, the Krommyonian sow. None is
properly described, but we know from later sources, especially Plutarch's
Life of Theseus, that each had a particular *modus operandi*, and in most
instances Theseus simply turned the tables on him, dispatching his opponent
with the same means he had earlier used on his unsuspecting victims.

Better than any late author, however, is a rich series of Athenian sculptures and vase-paintings that record all five encounters and one omitted by
Bacchylides. The representations start a good generation before the poem, at
the end of the sixth century, and continue throughout the fifth. From the
very beginning they present these deeds as a cycle, quite different, say, from
the twelve labors of Herakles. The latter were set in many far-flung locations
and took place over a period of time. They are treated by the vase-painters as
discrete episodes, and rarely are more than two combined on a single vase.
For Theseus, however, they created a unique narrative technique, juxtaposing up to half-a-dozen scenes to suggest, as does Bacchylides, that they all
took place in rapid succession. A comparison of the so-called "cycle cups"
from before, during, and after the time of Bacchylides suggests how the
Theseus myth evolved in the course of the fifth century.

Figure 76 Deeds of Theseus: Prokrustes, Kerkyon, Minotaur. Attic red-figure cup
related to the Painter of Louvre G36, side A. London, British Museum E36. Ca. 510.

111

One of the very earliest, still before 500, is a rather fine cup in London (Figs. 76 and 77). Five episodes cover the two exterior surfaces, but the overlap with Bacchylides' five is only partial. Perhaps the easiest to recognize are Kerkyon, in the middle of Side A (see Fig. 76) and the sow, at the right on Side B (see Fig. 77). Kerkyon was a master wrestler – Bacchylides refers to his palaestra, or wrestling-school – and Theseus simply outwrestled him in what is usually depicted as a fair fight. His handling of the sow (actually depicted as a male in this scene) is rather unorthodox here, for instead of simply killing it, he has tied up the legs and drags it off, as if planning a barbecue. A curious detail is the presence of Hermes, waving his kerykeion toward Theseus. On the left of Side A, Theseus attacks with an axe a huge man clinging in his death-throes to a rock. A deep wound in his side gushes blood. The axe tells us he must be Prokrustes, although we miss the famous bed, which is in fact included on a cup contemporary with this one.

Thus far our painter and Bacchylides could be working from a common source; but with the inclusion of two other combats, the painter seems to get derailed from his proper subject. On Side B, Theseus has lassoed a magnificent bull, bound its feet, and prepares to lead it away. From Plutarch we learn that, soon after his arrival in Athens, Theseus, eager for new challenges, went out to Marathon, in eastern Attika, captured this enormous bull, and drove it home to sacrifice in Athens. The pairing of bull and boar on our cup makes good artistic sense, but thematically the bull is out of place, since this deed was not part of that first journey to Athens. Similarly,

Figure 77 Deeds of Theseus: bull, sow. Side B of the cup shown in Fig. 76 (p. 111).

the last pairing on Side A (at the extreme right) has Theseus attacking the Minotaur – the creature, with its bull's head and tail on a man's body, is unmistakable. However, this episode lies even further in the future, once Theseus is well established as the Athenian prince but anxious to serve his people by undertaking the dangerous mission to Crete. We must conclude that for the painter, working without poetic models like Bacchylides 18 (or from an earlier poem, an epic *Theseid*), the "deeds of Theseus" comprised a wide assortment, from which he felt free to make a selection that best suited his artistic purpose. The slaying of the Minotaur already had a long history in Greek art when this cup was made, and the Marathonian bull is also attested in earlier black-figure, while the episodes on the road from Troizen are all new as of about 510. It was only natural that these first red-figure painters combined the old with the new, each creating his own distinctive Theseus cycle.

Some decades later, when a contemporary of Bacchylides took up the story of Theseus, the disposition of the individual episodes on his cup suggests a keen awareness of the sequence of the hero's early career (Figs. 78–80). The tondo, which in the earliest cycle cups is always unrelated to Theseus, is now reserved for the Minotaur (see Fig. 78). Grasping the beast by one horn, Theseus decapitates it with a swift stroke of his sword. Cup-painters had by this time become masters at adapting their two-figure compositions to the circular surface, and this is no exception. The collapsing Minotaur's body follows the curve, while Theseus is able to brace himself with both feet against the border for the *coup de grâce*.

On the exterior, one whole side is devoted to the capture of the Marathonian bull (see Fig. 79). Kneeling into the bull to keep it pinned to the ground, Theseus will truss it with his rope. Two nearly identical women watch in amazement. They might be called local nymphs of the Marathon region, but in truth their main function is to fill out the scene and heighten the excitement of this daring feat. Turning to the other side of the cup (see Fig. 80), we find three of the deeds on the road to Athens, including the two from Bacchylides that we missed on the earlier cup. At the left, Theseus charges a wild-looking opponent, wielding in his back hand an axe. It is, in fact, the same weapon he uses against Prokrustes at the other end of the frieze, but this first opponent is identified by another attribute, the long branches of a pine tree that he holds aloft. Sinis would later acquire the nickname "Pinebender" on account of his favorite trick, attaching his victims' limbs to branches compressed like a spring, then releasing.

The middle of this side is filled with a bold depiction of the encounter with Skiron. It was his nasty habit to compel passers-by to wash his feet (the bronze basin is visible on the ground), then kick them over a steep cliff. The cliff is here impressionistically rendered as a huge rock, but Skiron's

Figure 78 Theseus killing the Minotaur. Attic red-figure cup attributed to the Dokimasia Painter, interior. Florence, Museo Nazionale 70800. Ca. 470.

Figure 79 Theseus subduing the Marathonian bull. Side B of the cup shown in Fig. 78 (above).

Figure 80 Deeds of Theseus: Sinis, Skiron, Prokrustes. Side A of the cup shown in Fig. 78 (p. 114).

contorted position as he is upended by Theseus effectively conveys the vertiginous feeling of his downward plunge.

The three picture surfaces of the cup thus give the painter the opportunity to create a cycle that is truly sequential, from the journey to Athens to the first deed in Attika (the bull), to the culmination of Theseus' exploits, on Crete. The impression of scene-changes is particularly supported by clothing Theseus in a short pleated garment for his fight with the Minotaur, while earlier he had fought in the nude. At the same time, little details (such as his pointed traveling-cap, or pilos, that hangs in the background of all three scenes) remind us – as if there were any doubt – that our hero is always the same.

Theseus' outfit, as Bacchylides describes it, has aroused much interest for its remarkable specificity and unexpected geographical associations. The painters prefer to show him heroically nude, although this is not necessarily incompatible with the poet. He faces his enemies stripped for action, but would logically don his best outfit for his entry into Athens. In other respects there is close agreement between poet and painters, especially in the emphasis they both place on Theseus' extreme youth. However, while Bacchylides stresses his enormous physical strength, the vase-painters seem to attribute his success more to skill and determination. The ivory-hilted sword is, of course, indispensable, not only because Theseus makes good use of it, but because it will be the proof of his identity in Athens.

When we once again move down some thirty to forty years, we find Athenian cup-painters again looking for new ways to translate the notion of a cycle into visual terms (Fig. 81). Cycle (Greek *kyklos*) means "circle," and here, by using the full interior, the painter has created a true cycle, with no beginning or end or handles to interrupt. He has reintegrated the Marathonian bull into the cycle, only now at a later stage of that episode, as Theseus drives it across Attika and home to Athens. A few other elements show the artist's familiarity with the, by now, long pictorial tradition, as well as the urge to innovate. Thus, Prokrustes' bed and the old woman

Figure 81 Center: Theseus drags the Minotaur from the Labyrinth; *frieze*: deeds of Theseus (clockwise from top), Kerkyon, Prokrustes, Skiron, bull, Sinis, sow. Interior of Attic red-figure cup, attributed to the Kodros Painter. London, British Museum E84. Ca. 440–430.

alongside the sow (named "Phaia" in literary sources) are both standard features by now, while the use of Skiron's foot-basin as a weapon is a new feature, added about mid-century. Once again the Minotaur is given pride of place in the middle of the tondo, but with an ingenious twist. The beast is not quite dead, and Theseus drags it out of a Labyrinth whose architecture is cleverly rendered as a combination of standard Doric order with an ornate, patterned doorway. On the outside of the cup, the painter repeated the entire cycle but, curiously, with very little variation from the interior. The effect is one of overkill.

Bacchylides 17: Theseus at the bottom of the sea

The slaying of the Minotaur was not only the centerpiece of Theseus' career as a young hero, but also the deed that first transcended his local importance to Athens and put him in the category of the great monster-slayers of Greek tradition, alongside Herakles, Perseus, and Bellerophon. Artists of all periods and far from Athens counted the Minotaur among their favorite subjects. Yet when Bacchylides presented his own version of the Cretan adventure at the Delian festival, he chose to ignore the Minotaur entirely and instead to celebrate a very different aspect of Theseus' heroic nature. In so doing, he helped to reshape much of the mythological tradition while creating a literary work of magical beauty.

Archaic tradition knew that Theseus had once paid a visit to the undersea home of his divine father Poseidon – an Attic vase made in Bacchylides' youth attests to this – but it may have been the poet's own idea to set that episode within the context of the journey to Crete. Again, all sources agreed that the Athenians had to send seven youths and seven maidens at regular intervals as tribute to King Minos and that Theseus volunteered to go with them. Only Bacchylides, however, imagined that Minos came personally in his own ship to fetch the victims.

When, on board ship, Minos starts to molest one of the Athenian girls, for whom Theseus feels responsible, this sets the stage for a dramatic confrontation between the impetuous young prince and the arrogant barbarian king. Both claim descent from the Olympian gods, Minos from Zeus and Theseus from Poseidon. A thunderbolt from Zeus, coming right on cue, proves Minos' claim. He challenges Theseus to prove his own by retrieving a gold ring cast into the sea. With the reckless confidence of youth, Theseus immediately plunges overboard, and Minos, believing he has seen the last of this young pest, orders the ship to sail on:

> The racing keel sped on, northwind
>   rushing from the stern,
>   and all that godlike group
> of young Athenians trembled as

their hero leapt into the sea.
　　Tears fell from tender eyes
　　that watched this rough necessity
but sea-bred dolphins came
　　and swiftly carried Theseus
to his hippic father's realm.
　　He stepped into the hall
　　of the divinities and there he saw
　　the fabled girls of Nereus
　　and was afraid, for lights
　　leapt from their shining limbs
like sparks, and strands of gold
　　wound through their hair
in diadems as, circling in their play,
　　they danced on sea-wet toes.
He saw as well his father's wife,
august, wide-glancing Amphitrite,
　　mistress of the lovely house.
She wrapped a purple cloak about him,

then placed upon his uncut curls
the perfect rose-dark wreath
that on her wedding day
sly Aphrodite once gave her to wear.
Nothing that the gods desire
should be beyond the faith of thinking man!
He showed himself beside the ship's
light prow, and oh he checked
the Cnossian king's plans now
as he rose up, unwet, out of that sea,
a marvel to them all!
　　　　　　　　　　Bacchylides 17.90–123

This beautiful poem has a logic of its own which has baffled many modern commentators. Theseus' miraculous re-emergence from the sea (not even wet!) surely proves his paternity, but the gold ring is simply forgotten and never again mentioned. And although he has certainly been in his "hippic father's realm" ("hippic" because of Poseidon's close association with horses), he seems not to have met his divine father at all, but only the ladies of the house.

Such are the prerogatives of the poet, but painters are usually more literal-minded. The ring itself interested them even less than it did Bacchylides, yet when it came to Poseidon's undersea palace they could be quite precise. The finest rendering is on a red-figure cup so close in date to Bacchylides that it is hard to say if the painter would have known the poem or not (Figs. 82–84). In either case, he has created his own vision of Theseus' Cretan journey that is even broader in scope than Bacchylides'.

Poseidon's palace is a fine Doric structure of suitably grand proportions (see Fig. 82). The god himself directs the action with a gesture of his outstretched hand (the other holds a particularly handsome trident), but the painter has lavished his greatest care on the figure of Triton. This Man Friday of the deep, Poseidon's all-round factotum, is, despite his enormous size and scaly body, a gentle and benevolent creature, as we see from the care with which he prepares to escort Theseus back to the surface. The artist has dispensed with Bacchylides' dolphins in favor of Triton, who had a long and honored tradition in Attic vase-painting. Three Nereids prepare a festive send-off for the young prince, including libations poured from shallow metal phialai. Theseus' boyishness is deliberately emphasized by the contrast with the huge and stately Triton.

In Bacchylides it is Poseidon's consort, Amphitrite, who plays the key role in welcoming Theseus, and so too the painter has highlighted that moment by placing it in the cup tondo (see Fig. 83). The hero has already received from her the purple cloak, draped casually over his arms, and now she presents him with a wreath. The "uncut curls" of the youth who has not yet reached the age of an ephebe (about 18) are clearly shown in nearly all representations of Theseus in this period. Often, as on this cup, he has rolled up his long hair in the back or fastened it with a fillet.

The other frieze on the outside of the cup completes the cycle of three Theseus scenes (see Fig. 84), yet despite its specificity, it remains an enigma. Theseus, with drawn sword, stands before his (and Athens') patroness, Athena, while four women frame this central pair, offering gifts: a sprig, a wreath, and a fillet. Two Doric columns suggest that once again we are in a palatial setting. At least three different interpretations have been offered: first, Theseus' first arrival in Athens, from Troizen, welcomed by the goddess and the women of the city; second, his departure from Athens for Crete; or, third, his triumphal return to Athens after the sojourn on Crete. The choice depends largely on one's reading of the various gestures, an imprecise science at best. Gestures are a culture's unspoken language, and for the ancient Greeks we have no native informants. Is Athena's out-stretched hand, for example, a gesture of valediction, sending the hero out on his mission, or of greeting? Do the uplifted hands of the woman at left express excitement at Theseus' happy return or fear for his safety as he departs? A different approach would be to ask which moment would fit best into the painter's tripartite Theseus cycle. Certainly not the first, which is unrelated to the Cretan adventure. Of the other two, both would be suitable. The dilemma remains.

If the painter of the New York cup was inspired by the Theseus cycle cups to create his own kind of cycle, a contemporary of his adapted the same

119

Figure 82 Theseus in the Palace of Poseidon at the bottom of the sea. Attic red-figure cup, attributed to the Briseis Painter, side A. New York, Metropolitan Museum 53.11.4. Ca. 480.

Figure 83 Theseus receiving gifts from Amphitrite. Interior of the cup shown in Fig. 82 (above).

Figure 84 Athena sending Theseus out to Crete (?). Side B of the cup shown in Fig. 82 (p. 120).

story to the monumental grandeur of the column-krater (Fig. 85). In this type of narrative, especially popular in the years after 480, all the figures line up paratactically, and each one's importance is reflected in his or her position. Thus the middle of the five figures is Poseidon, and the focal point of the whole composition is the handshake between him and Theseus. In rather mundane, yet unmistakably clear fashion, the painter has reduced the message of Bacchylides' poem to a single gesture – the handshake – as the symbol of Theseus' divine paternity. Behind him stands Amphitrite, holding the wreath as on the New York cup (see Fig. 83). At the other side, a Nereid, pouring a libation, exchanges glances with her father Nereus, the Old Man of the Sea. He fits into this dignified gathering much better than the rather exotic Triton. The sober scene may have lost the magic of Bacchylides or the cup in New York, but its message to an Athenian viewer in the aftermath of the Persian Wars comes across loud and clear: Theseus is Poseidon's son; we Athenians, descendants of Theseus, drove back the Persian fleet with Poseidon's help and, again with his help, will rule the Aegean.

It is difficult to dissociate the burst of interest in Theseus' visit to Poseidon, both in vase-painting and in Bacchylides 17, from the creation of the Delian League, under Athens' leadership, in the 470s. However, myths also have a life of their own, so it should not surprise us if, after a hiatus of fifty years, the subject reappears on a magnificent calyx-krater of the last years of the Peloponnesian War (see Fig. 86). In keeping with artistic developments of the intervening half-century, the composition is now multi-level, enabling the painter to transport us more convincingly to the depths of the sea. Indeed, at the top left, the chariot of Helios is just emerging from the waves for his daily journey across the sky. Theseus has just arrived from his ship (its oars, not visible in this view, are shown above the left handle) and is "delivered" by Triton into the presence of his regal step-mother Amphitrite. She has prepared for him a rich crown of leaves and berries. Poseidon, playing the man of the house, reclines on his couch and shows no inclination to get up and greet his son. The curious ménage also includes several Nereids at the upper right, unimpressed by the new arrival, and an Eros, mixing wine and water in a big krater. The casually domestic quality of the whole setting is reminiscent of Attic tragedy's propensity in these same years for bringing the Olympian gods down to the level of bourgeois Athenian society. The scene was inspired not by a tragedy, however, but by a different kind of performance. The two elaborate tripods that appear perched on columns allude to a victory in a dithyrambic contest; but it was probably not Bacchylides' dithyramb – rather one by a poet of the late fifth century of which we have no other trace.

Figure 85 Theseus meeting Poseidon. Attic red-figure column-krater, attributed to the Harrow Painter. Harvard University, Arthur M. Sackler Museum 1960.339. Ca. 470.

Figure 86 Theseus received by Amphitrite and Poseidon. Red-figure calyx-krater attributed to the Kadmos Painter. Bologna, Museo Civico 303. Ca. 410.

4

DRAMA

Greek drama was said to have originated with a performance staged in Athens by one Thespis in the year 538 B.C.. We know nothing of what this first performance was like, but it is a safe assumption that it bore little resemblance to the surviving plays of the three great fifth-century trage-dians. Aeschylus, earliest of the three, was probably born about 525 (he fought at the Battle of Marathon in 490) and could well have been presenting plays by 500 or soon after, yet the first one we can securely date is the *Persians* of 472. Thus Attic tragedy, as we now have it, is essentially a Classical genre, developing in the years after the Persian invasion of 480/79 and ending with the late works of Sophocles and Euripides, in the last decade of the fifth century. Although Pindar and Bacchylides might well have witnessed productions of their contemporary Aeschylus, whether the orig-inals in Athens or revivals in Sicily, it is fair to say that their victory odes and dithyrambs represent the end of an Archaic tradition in Greek poetry, while the playwright heralds the creation of a new Classical genre.

This is not to say, however, that the new genre broke with the past in its choice of subject-matter. The *Persians* is the only extant tragedy that draws for its subject on recent historical events; all the others treat myths that were well known to the Athenian audience from earlier epic and lyric verse. Aeschylus' plays were called in antiquity "slices from the banquet of Homer." The same could be said of Euripides and Sophocles, if by "Homer" we understand the whole sweep of the Epic Cycle. In fact, this is the only way to interpret this famous phrase, since neither among the preserved plays of Aeschylus, nor among those of the other two tragedians, is there one based on an episode told in the *Iliad* or *Odyssey*. This may be partly an accident of preservation, but it also suggests that the playwrights tended to avoid direct borrowing from Homer and instead exploited epic material that was not as closely connected with the famous bard.

AESCHYLUS

In 458 Aeschylus presented a cycle of three plays – the only complete trilogy we have preserved – on the family of Agamemnon. It is called the *Oresteia*, because as the trilogy unfolds, it focuses increasingly on the fortunes of Agamemnon's son Orestes, culminating in the last play in his trial for the murder of his mother. Murder is indeed a leitmotiv of this trilogy – and of the visual tradition that both preceded and followed it – murder and the inherited curse that plagued the family through the generations.

Agamemnon: the murder of Agamemnon

The murder of Agamemnon on his return from Troy, plotted by his wife, Klytaimestra, and her paramour, Aegisthus (Agamemnon's cousin), was a famous story long before Aeschylus dramatized it. In the *Odyssey* alone, Homer tells the story several times and twice brings on the ghost of Agamemnon to lament his own murder at the hands of his treacherous wife (11.418–26; 24.199–202). Once he holds Aegisthus responsible for planning and carrying out the deed, "with the help of my accursed wife" (11.407–10). Nestor also seems to believe it was Aegisthus who plotted the murder (3.261). Yet elsewhere Homer implies that Klytaimestra acted alone. The setting was a banquet in the hall of the palace, and the carnage included some of Agamemnon's men, as well as Kassandra, the Trojan princess brought home as his prize. In Agamemnon's description to Odysseus, the bloody scene prefigures that of the slaughtered suitors later in the poem.

There were other, now lost, poetic versions of the death of Agamemnon between Homer and Aeschylus – one long one by Stesichoros, for example. The scene of the crime was shifted, at some point, from the banquet hall to the bath, as we find it in Aeschylus. Even more importantly, as a dramatist Aeschylus had to sort out the ambiguous tradition about what role each of the two conspirators played. Aegisthus is relegated to a clearly subsidiary position; he does not even appear on stage until some time after the murder and then can only claim to have helped plot the deed, to avenge Atreus' insult to his father Thyestes (the famous meal of his own children's flesh). The killing of Agamemnon was Klytaimestra's deed alone, as she herself confirms for us as she stands, covered with blood, over his corpse and that of Kassandra and defiantly addresses the chorus of elders:

> Much have I said before to serve necessity,
> but I will take no shame now to unsay it all.
> How else could I, arming hate against hateful men
> disguised in seeming tenderness, fence high the nets
> of ruin beyond overleaping? Thus to me
> the conflict born of ancient bitterness is not

125

a thing new thought upon, but pondered deep in time.
I stand now where I struck him down. The thing is done.
Thus have I wrought, and I will not deny it now.
That he might not escape nor beat aside his death,
as fishermen cast their huge circling nets, I spread
deadly abundance of rich robes, and caught him fast.
I struck him twice. In two great cries of agony
he buckled at the knees and fell. When he was down
I struck him the third blow, in thanks and reverence
to Zeus the lord of dead men underneath the ground.
Thus he went down, and the life struggled out of him;
and as he died he spattered me with the dark red
and violent driven rain of bitter savored blood
to make me glad, as gardens stand among the showers
of God in glory at the birthtime of the buds.

These being the facts, elders of Argos assembled here,
be glad, if it be your pleasure; but for me, I glory.
Were it religion to pour wine above the slain,
this man deserved, more than deserved, such sacrament.
He filled our cup with evil things unspeakable
and now himself come home has drunk it to the dregs.

Agamemnon 1372–98

Her weapon is still the sword, as in Homer, but the net in which she trapped her victim is new – at least in extant literature. Like all murders in Greek tragedy, this one takes place offstage; but Klytaimestra's description is so graphic, as is the horrific sight of the bodies with her astride them, that Aeschylus leaves little to the imagination.

The pictorial tradition of the death of Agamemnon begins quite early, before the end of the seventh century, and in an unexpected part of Greece, the island of Crete (Fig. 87). A mold-made terracotta relief concentrates the three principals into a moment of astonishing vigor and clarity, despite the somewhat clumsy figured style at this early date. Agamemnon is characterized as king by the elaborate chair in which he sits and the long spear or scepter held diagonally across his chest. Aegisthus grasps the spear in one hand, to disable the victim, and, in an extraordinary gesture, with all his strength holds down Agamemnon's head with his right hand. Thus immobilized, Agamemnon cannot resist as Klytaimestra plunges a dagger into his chest.

What gives the scene much of its immediacy and power is the frontality of the three faces, such a rarity in later Greek art (cf. Figs. 124 and 125). It is as if the fatal moment is frozen forever in time by the artist's snapshot. The murder is definitely a joint effort, but the more active role is Klytaimestra's.

The tight compression of three figures into a rectangular frame whose

Figure 87 Death of Agamemnon. Terracotta plaque from Gortyn. Heraklion, Archaeological Museum 11512. Ca. 630–610.

edges they threaten to burst is a peculiarly Archaic form, which recurs, on a smaller scale, on some bronze shield-bands of the sixth century. Such panels in low relief were often linked together, forming the strap of a big round shield. A well preserved example, from Olympia, has much in common with the Cretan relief, except that Agamemnon's throne has been removed (Fig. 88). Instead, he staggers from the wound that Klytaimestra has inflicted, as Aegisthus seizes him in a kind of wrestling hold. The spear would not have suited this composition, so the artist has placed it to one side.

On the matter of who killed Agamemnon, all texts and images have thus far been in agreement in giving Klytaimestra the more active role. It is then all the more surprising to turn to the most celebrated of all representations and find Aegisthus as the clear perpetrator (Fig. 89). This splendid krater is unique in combining the deaths of Agamemnon and Aegisthus on a single vase (cf. Fig. 96); but even if we had only the front of the vase, it would completely alter our understanding of the myth.

The date of the vase is most probably ten to fifteen years earlier than Aeschylus' *Oresteia*, and therefore it represents one version of the story current in Athens when Aeschylus set to work. Here we learn, first, that the net in which Agamemnon was caught is not an invention of Aeschylus, but

Figure 88 Death of Agamemnon. Bronze shield-band. Olympia Museum B1654. Ca. 575–550.

Figure 89 Death of Agamemnon. Attic red-figure calyx-krater, attributed to the Dokimasia Painter, side A. Boston, Museum of Fine Arts 63.1246. Ca. 470.

Figure 90 Kassandra fleeing from the murder of Agamemnon. Handle zone of the calyx-krater shown in Fig. 89 (p. 128).

must have been borrowed by him from an earlier source. The combination of the sheer net and the slender, nude body underneath makes this Agamemnon look far more vulnerable than in the Archaic representations. There can be no doubt that in this version Aegisthus delivers the fatal blow with his sword, even if Klytaimestra comes to his aid wielding an axe (not visible here). The same weapon was in Aeschylus' mind too, as we shall see, only he transferred it to a later stage of the story. Two more excited women, plausibly identified as Agamemnon's daughters, Electra and Chrysothemis, are stock figures on vases of this period, although they are usually stirred up by an erotic chase rather than a murder.

One last figure belongs to the scene, although we only see her by turning the vase to the handle zone (Fig. 90). She, too, flees in distress, arms in the air, but is otherwise quite different from the women of Agamemnon's family: smaller, differently dressed, with close-cropped hair. She must be Kassandra, whose distress is even more frantic than the others' since she foresees her own murder following close upon that of Agamemnon. Her short hair is typical of slave-girls in Greek art; although born of royalty, Kassandra has come as a slave to Mycenae. As we noted, Kassandra's death at the hands of Klytaimestra had been associated with Agamemnon's already in Homer (*Odyssey* 11.422). There is a separate iconographic tradition in Attic vase-painting of Klytaimestra striking Kassandra down with an axe. We need only "unroll" our krater from handle to handle in order to grasp the double murder taking place: Klytaimestra charges at Kassandra, axe in hand, even as Aegisthus dispatches Agamemnon. There is a sexual symmetry of attackers and victims, as well as the visual symmetry of a perfectly balanced composition.

Libation Bearers: Electra and Orestes at the tomb of Agamemnon

When the second play of Aeschylus' trilogy opens, some years have passed since the murder of Agamemnon. Klytaimestra and Aegisthus live openly as man and wife and rulers of Argos. Her daughter Electra, loyal to the memory of her father, spends her days bringing offerings to his tomb, accompanied by the female attendants who give the play its title, and praying for the return of her brother Orestes. Only a boy at the time of Agamemnon's return from Troy, he had been sent away to friends by Klytaimestra, lest he prove an inconvenience to her plot. Orestes does, of course, return, finally, together with his trusted friend Pylades. One of the favorite dramatic devices of Greek tragedy was the anagnorisis, or recognition of two people, usually close relatives, long separated. Aeschylus may have helped popularize this device with his famous scene (famous enough to be gently parodied by Euripides), in which Orestes and Electra meet at their father's tomb. Orestes, from his hiding-place, has observed the somber ritual and deduced the identity of his sister. The slow and emotional recognition, then, is all on her side:

> But see, here is another sign. Footprints are here.
> The feet that made them are alike, and look like mine.
> There are two sets of footprints: of the man who gave
> his hair, and one who shared the road with him. I step
> where he has stepped, and heelmarks, and the space between
> his heel and toe are like the prints I make. Oh, this
> is torment, and my wits are going.

Orestes comes from his place of concealment

Orestes. Pray for what is to come, and tell the gods that they have brought your former prayers to pass. Pray for success.

Electra. Upon what ground? What have I won yet from the gods?

Orestes. You have come in sight of all you long since prayed to see.

Electra. How did you know what man was subject of my prayer?

Orestes. I know about Orestes, how he stirred your heart.

Electra. Yes; but how am I given an answer to my prayers?

Orestes. Look at me. Look for no one closer to you than I.

Electra. Is this some net of treachery, friend, you catch me in?

Orestes. Then I must be contriving plots against myself.

Electra. It is your pleasure to laugh at my unhappiness.

Orestes. I only mock my own then, if I laugh at you.

Electra. Are you really Orestes? Can I call you by that name?

Orestes. You see my actual self and are slow to learn. And yet
you saw this strand of hair I cut in sign of grief
and shuddered with excitement, for you thought you saw
me, and again when you were measuring my tracks.
Now lay the severed strand against where it was cut
and see how well your brother's hair matches my head.
Look at this piece of weaving, the work of your hand
with its blade strokes and figured design of beasts. No, no,
control yourself, and do not lose your head for joy.

Libation Bearers 205–33

The use of special tokens to bring about or confirm a recognition is, of
course, much older than Aeschylus. Eurykleia, the nurse, recognizes
Odysseus by the scar on his thigh, and the disguised Odysseus describes to
Penelope a golden brooch she once gave him. However, Aeschylus outdoes
them by introducing no fewer than three tokens: a lock of Orestes' hair, left
earlier at the tomb, with its genetic similarity to Electra's; the size and shape
of his footprint; and a garment once embroidered for him by his sister.

Later in the fifth century both Sophocles and Euripides wrote plays
entitled *Electra* that recount the same events as the *Libation Bearers*, includ-

Figure 91 Electra at the tomb of Agamemnon. Attic red-figure skyphos, attributed
to the Penelope Painter, side A. Copenhagen, National Museum 597. Ca. 440–430.

131

ing the recognition at the tomb. For Sophocles the token is a signet ring that had belonged to Agamemnon, now worn by Orestes, while Euripides revives all three of Aeschylus' tokens – hair, footprint, and garment – although his Electra is not so easily persuaded.

When Athenian vase-painters start to depict Electra and Orestes at their father's tomb, it is often impossible to say which of the three dramatic versions they had in mind, or if indeed they are simply imagining this famous episode without reference to any specific play.

The earliest example is also the only one, in either Attic or South Italian, that uses the opposite sides of the vase to such good effect in capturing the dramatic suspense of the scene (Figs. 91 and 92). On one side, Electra ties a wreath around the tomb of her father, while an attendant stands at the ready with more wreaths and offerings of fruit. The tomb monument adapts a standard type in Athens of this period, a tall, slightly tapering shaft atop a stepped platform, crowned by a single large palmette. Agamemnon's name, or as much of it as will fit on the narrow stele, is written in imitation of a carved inscription. The two women are so absorbed in their task that they are oblivious of the two young men observing them from a discreet distance (see Fig. 92). Orestes and Pylades, virtual twins, are characterized as travelers by the chlamys fastened at the neck, petasos (broad-brimmed hat), and double spears.

In the fourth century, the scene at the tomb of Agamemnon makes a smooth transition from Athens to South Italy. One of the very last Attic red-figure painters of skill and imagination took up the subject about 390 (Fig. 93). The influence of the *Libation Bearers* is unmistakable, even if the

Figure 92 Orestes and Pylades. Side B of the skyphos shown in Fig. 91 (p. 131).

Figure 93 Orestes at the tomb of Agamemnon. Attic red-figure pelike, attributed to the Jena Painter. Exeter University. Ca. 390.

Figure 94 Orestes and Electra at the tomb of Agamemnon. Lucanian red-figure panathenaic amphora. Naples, Museo Nazionale 82140 (H 1775). Ca. 380.

moment he has created is not one that happens in the play. Orestes cuts off the lock of hair he will leave as an offering, watched by Pylades, who sits casually on the steps of the tomb. In Aeschylus, this is a private moment in which Orestes makes sure to be unobserved (except by Pylades, of course). Here, instead, the painter has filled out the scene with several women, one holding the water-jar used in funerary rituals, and a young man. We might have had doubts whether the girl with the close-cropped haircut of mourning and the hydria in her hand is really Electra, if the painter had not helpfully written her name above her. The artist's interest is less in dramatic tension or fidelity than in a well balanced composition whose subject is immediately recognized. The tomb itself is in principle of the same type as the earlier one, only the inscription has been wisely moved down to the steps, where Agamemnon's long name (given, quite properly, in the genitive case: "[tomb] of Agamemnon") can be spread out in nice big letters.

In Magna Graecia, where the favorite plays of the Attic tragedians were often revived in local productions, we expect to find vase-paintings more closely following the action of a play. So, for example, the scene on an Apulian amphora could well correspond to *Libation Bearers* 212, when Orestes suddenly emerges from his hiding-place to address Electra (Fig. 94). She is quite unaware of his presence as she sits on the tomb, caught up in melancholy reverie. As on the Attic skyphos (see Fig. 91), a single attendant serves as a kind of shorthand for the chorus. Pylades is appropriately small and inconspicuous, the better to show off the heroic epiphany of Orestes. The youth watching from the upper right is reminiscent of a similar figure on the Exeter pelike (see Fig. 93), but his identity is obscure, since the playwrights do not offer any clues to the presence of another male. His detachment from the action, on another plane, suggests that he could function as a geographical signpost, say Argos, in the form of a local hero. The tomb of Agamemnon has been streamlined, with the emphasis now put on the armor of the old warrior. A nice touch is the offering-vase, perched beside the stele, which mimics the shape of our vase, perhaps a form of self-advertisement on the part of potter or painter.

Libation Bearers: the death of Aegisthus

After the recognition of Orestes and Electra, the long middle section of *Libation Bearers* is given over to prayers and incantations, the conjuring of the ghost of Agamemnon to fortify his children in their resolve to kill both Klytaimestra and Aegisthus. But how to gain access to the heavily guarded palace? Orestes hits on a stratagem: to present himself at the gate as a messenger, bearing the sad tidings that Orestes is dead. This will at least pique the interest of those within sufficiently to gain him admittance and a private audience with Aegisthus. Klytaimestra is unaware of her lover's plight until it is too late:

Follower of Aegisthus. O sorrow, all is sorrow for our stricken lord.
Raise up again a triple cry of sorrow, for
Aegisthus lives no longer. Open there, open
quick as you may, and slide back the doorbars on the women's
gates. It will take the strength of a young arm, but not
to fight for one who is dead and done for. What use there?
Ahoy!
My cry is to the deaf and I babble in vain
at sleepers to no purpose. Klytaimestra, where
is she, does what? Her neck is on the razor's edge
and ripe for lopping, as she did to others before.

                                        Enter Klytaimestra

Klytaimestra. What is this, and why are you shouting in the house?

Follower. I tell you, he is alive and killing the dead.

Klytaimestra. Ah, so. You speak in riddles, but I read the rhyme.
We have been won with the treachery by which we slew.
Bring me quick, somebody, an ax to kill a man

                                        Exit follower

and we shall see if we can beat him before we
go down – so far gone are we in this wretched fight.

                        Enter Orestes and Pylades with swords drawn

Orestes. You next: the other one in there has had enough.

Klytaimestra. Beloved, strong Aegisthus, are you dead indeed?

Orestes. You love your man, then? You shall lie in the same grave
with him, and never be unfaithful even in death.

                                        Libation Bearers 875–95

It is clearly the murder of Klytaimestra that constitutes the dramatic
climax of the play, that of Aegisthus only a brief and unseen prelude. Yet
when we look for representations in Archaic and Classical art of this most
famous case of matricide, we are surprised by its absence, while the death of
Aegisthus has a long and rich visual tradition. How are we to understand
this discrepancy? The Homeric *Odyssey* again offers a clue to pre-
Aeschylean ways of thinking. As Nestor recounts the story (*Odyssey* 3.304–
10), Klytaimestra's death is merely an afterthought; the gist is that, after
ruling over Mycenae for seven years, the usurper Aegisthus was slain by
Orestes, who thus exacted vengeance for the murder of Agamemnon. In
other words, in both instances the murder is more political than personal,
more about legitimate or illegitimate seizure of power than a family curse.
The implication is that Orestes will now assume his rightful role as ruler of
Mycenae. Power and kingship are matters for men to fight out, hence
Klytaimestra's often marginal role in the pre-Aeschylean *Oresteia*.

135

Aeschylus' most radical innovation was to take Klytaimestra seriously as a political figure, a point she herself has difficulty getting across to the old-fashioned chorus of male elders. It is she who both plans and executes the murder of Agamemnon, she who wields power in Mycenae, and who therefore is the principal target of Orestes' revenge. Aegisthus is consistently relegated to the subsidiary, or "female," role.

Not so the artistic tradition, which focused exclusively on Orestes as regicide, rather than matricide. It starts before the middle of the seventh century, with a much discussed vase that almost certainly depicts the death of Aegisthus (Fig. 95). In a curious way, the scene anticipates aspects of Aeschylus' dramatization: Aegisthus is dispatched first, while Klytaimestra is seized by the awful realization that her fate is close at hand. As we may recall from the blinding of Polyphemos (see Figs. 30 and 31), the Proto-Attic style, whatever its artistic limitations, could pack tremendous narrative power and expressiveness into a simple composition; the visual contrast of the black Orestes and white Aegisthus also finds a good parallel on the Eleusis Amphora.

After a hiatus of a century and a half, the subject of Aegisthus' murder re-entered the repertoire of Attic vase-painting at the turn of the sixth century, perhaps, as some have suggested, because the motif of the slaying of a tyrant recalled the murder of the Athenian tyrant Hipparchos in 514 by the "Tyrannicides" Harmodios and Aristogeiton. The version on the krater in Boston would be a typical member of the extensive series in Late Archaic and Early Classical red-figure (Fig. 96), were it not for the fact that it shares the vase with the unique depiction of the death of Agamemnon (see Figs. 89 and 90).

The compositions of the two sides of this krater in fact have much in common, each dominated by a striding, sword-wielding attacker moving to the right. The similarities, of course, underscore the irony that the confident aggressor of the earlier scene has become the helpless victim of the later. Aegisthus has even aged appropriately in the intervening seven years, from a smartly dressed and coiffed mature man into a somewhat dissolute-looking, aging tyrant. The lyre he holds has been much discussed, whether it is the result of confusion with scenes of the murder of a musician (Orpheus), or was deliberately included, perhaps to reflect the pleasures of the complacent king or the victim's utter surprise and defenselessness at the moment of the attack.

The presence of essentially the same axe-wielding Klytaimestra on both sides is also not without its irony, as she too turns from aggressor to victim. In the climactic scene of the *Libation Bearers*, she presumably never does get hold of the axe for which she calls; here she has it, but little good will it do her. Lastly, the figure thought to be Electra, a young woman with flowing hair and outstretched right hand, is virtually identical on both sides. This means, however, that the same gesture must be interpreted in two quite

136

Figure 95 Death of Aegisthus. Proto-Attic krater, attributed to the Ram Jug Painter. Once Berlin A32. Ca. 675–650.

Figure 96 Death of Aegisthus. Side B of Attic red-figure calyx-krater shown in Fig. 89 (p. 128).

Figure 97 Death of Aegisthus: Klytaimestra with axe. Above handle of Attic red-figure calyx-krater, attributed to the Aegisthus Painter. Malibu, J. Paul Getty Museum 88.AE.66. Ca. 470–460.

different ways, once conveying distress and the futile attempt to stop the murder of her father, once joy and encouragement of the deadly blow struck by her brother. Perhaps other identifications should be considered.

There is thus a certain paradox about the design of this extraordinary vase. On the one hand, the very juxtaposition of the two murders represents an unusually thoughtful and original confrontation with the Orestes myth. Emily Vermeule, in her now classic publication of the krater, was convinced that this was conceivable only if the painter had witnessed Aeschylus' trilogy from the audience in 458, although most scholars maintain that dating the vase any later than 470/65 would do great violence to the chronology of Attic red-figure so painstakingly worked out by Sir John Beazley and others. If the krater *does* predate 458, then it is even more to the painter's credit to have anticipated the central paradox of killer turned victim; as Aeschylus' chorus asks, "Must he give blood for generations gone, die for those slain and in death pile up more death to come for the bloodshed?" (*Agamemnon* 1338–40). Yet for all his originality, the artist seems curiously bound by the repertoire of stock figure types that he inherited, which give his pictures a rather mannered look, like tableaux vivants rather than true action.

The Boston krater was thought by many to be the last word on the death of Aegisthus; but in the early 1980s yet another version came to light that in many ways overshadows it (Figs. 97–99). The comparison is not a fair one,

Figure 98 Death of Aegisthus: Orestes slays Aegisthus. Side A of the calyx-krater shown in Fig. 97 (p. 138).

but perhaps inevitable, since the two vases are contemporary and both calyx-kraters. While the Boston vase remains unique as an *Oresteia* cycle, the painter of the Getty vase, by spreading the one scene over the entire surface of a krater of enormous proportions, elevated it to a monumentality of scale and conception rarely seen in vase-painting. Because his figures are also less mannered than those of the Dokimasia Painter and less predictable, the scene has greater energy and immediacy.

The magnificent central group focuses on Aegisthus, the dandified tyrant in splendid long robes, flowing locks, and carefully tended long beard, seated on a suitably elegant throne (see Fig. 98). His posture is utterly credible, slipping off the throne under the impact of the sword plunged into his chest, but with his last bit of strength trying vainly with both hands to fend off Orestes. The young attacker is spectacularly nude, and his sudden turn of the head away from Aegisthus at the fatal moment is particularly arresting. At first it makes us think of depictions of Perseus decapitating Medusa, on whose face he dared not look; but then we notice the reason for Orestes' abrupt turn: he has suddenly become aware of his mother's approach, now wielding the axe with both hands, as if she really means business (see Fig. 97). Unfortunately for her, close on her heels is a mature man who slows her progress by grasping her shoulder with one hand and the axe-head with the other. From an earlier, inscribed version we know he is Talthybios, Agamemnon's herald in the *Iliad* (cf. Fig. 7), who is evidently

139

Figure 99 Death of Aegisthus: Electra (?). Above handle of the calyx-krater shown in Fig. 97 (p. 138).

still a family retainer loyal to his master's son Orestes. The young woman rushing in from the right recalls the two "Electras" in Boston, but the unusual gesture of the right hand to the forehead intensifies her excitement even further (see Fig. 99). The biggest surprise, however, is the appearance of a young woman between Orestes and his mother, holding a baby. Her simple outfit, close-cropped hair, and strange impassiveness in the midst of this horror all argue that she is not a family member, but rather a slave-girl or nurse. The baby, then, is the family member, most likely one of the two children born to Klytaimestra and Aegisthus.

Five figures fill the reverse of the vase, apparently three men and two women, although large chunks are missing. From their generalized dress, gestures, and poses we have the impression that the painter did not have names for them, but intended them as something like the tragic chorus, registering with alarm and excitement, but utter helplessness, the climactic act.

Once again we have, on the Getty krater, an approach to narrative that is highly dramatic, even theatrical in some ways, without, however, being dependent on a specific dramatic production or a pre-Aeschylean *Oresteia*. It is perhaps enough to recall that by the 470s, tragic performances in the Theatre of Dionysos were part of every Athenian citizen's experience, and even if the vase-painters among them chose surprisingly seldom to render what they had seen on stage, their store of visual imagery and notions of

Figures 100 and 101 Death of Aegisthus: Orestes slays Aegisthus. Apulian red-figure oinochoe attributed to the Wind Group. Paris, Louvre K320. Ca. 320.

story-telling cannot have remained unaffected. The Getty krater, in its monumentality, also reminds us of another source of inspiration, the art of large-scale fresco-painting, which came into its own in Athens in the generation after the Persian Wars. Among the great panoramic murals of epic derivation – a sack of Troy and a descent into the Underworld were two of the celebrated works by Polygnotos, the greatest of the fresco-painters – could have been an Oresteia that has left no trace in our written sources, only indirect reflections on the vases.

We may conclude with one Apulian version of the murder of Aegisthus, in part to make the point that, although these may look more "theatrical," thanks to elements of costume, sets, and props, they are in essence no more faithful to the plays themselves. On this oinochoe (Figs. 100 and 101), Aegisthus is the luxuriously attired king, caught by surprise as he sits on an ornate throne. Orestes plunges the sword into his chest, while Pylades grabs hold of the victim from behind. It is impossible to say how Aeschylus or his audience might have envisioned Pylades' involvement in the murder, since it took place off-stage in any case, but it is hard to imagine they thought of him as such an active participant. Rather, this is the contribution of a painter who liked the symmetrical composition of two striding figures attacking a seated one. Similarly, the Fury who appears behind Pylades has more to do with the need to fill out the composition than with dramatic logic. If this were the murder of Klytaimestra, then the sudden appearance of a Fury would be appropriate. To say that the Fury here is a proleptic reference to the impending death of Klytaimestra would be an overly subtle interpretation.

In order to find a case where it can plausibly be argued that vase-painters *did* go directly from the Theatre of Dionysos to their studios and took brush in hand, we must turn to the final play of Aeschylus' *Oresteia* trilogy.

Eumenides: Orestes at Delphi

The play opens in Apollo's sanctuary at Delphi, where Orestes has come seeking refuge after the murders. It was natural that he come here, not only because in Greek tradition murderers regularly sought expiation of their crime at Delphi, but because it was Apollo himself who had laid on Orestes the heavy charge to kill his own mother in order to avenge his father's death. Pylades had reminded Orestes of this at his one moment of hesitation (*Libation Bearers* 900–2), a single burst of speech in an otherwise silent role. The blood-guilt with which Orestes is tainted is not limited to some abstract, religious construct, but manifests itself as the Furies, or Erinyes, who hound him everywhere he goes and have followed him here to Delphi. We have already seen that, in her most basic form, the Fury could be imagined as a snake, attacking Ixion (see Fig. 59). Just how Aeschylus – or his costume designer – pictured the Furies is unclear, but they were evidently horrific enough to cause pregnant women in Aeschylus' audience to miscarry (as we are told), and to utterly unhinge Apollo's priestess, who stumbles upon them asleep at the opening of the play:

> Things terrible to tell and for the eyes to see
> terrible drove me out again from Loxias' house
> so that I have no strength and cannot stand on springing
> feet, but run with hands' help and my legs have no speed.
> An old woman afraid is nothing: a child, no more.
>
>   See, I am on my way to the wreath-hung recess
> and on the centrestone I see a man with god's
> defilement on him postured in the suppliant's seat
> with blood dripping from his hands and from a new-drawn
>   sword,
> holding too a branch that had grown high on an olive
> tree, decorously wrapped in a great tuft of wool,
> and the fleece shone. So far, at least, I can speak clear.
>
>   In front of this man slept a startling company
> of women lying all upon the chairs. Or not
> women, I think I call them rather gorgons, only
> not gorgons either, since their shape is not the same.
> I saw some creatures painted in a picture once,
> who tore the food from Phineus, only these had no
> wings, that could be seen; they are black and utterly
> repulsive, and they snore with breath that drives one back.
> From their eyes drips the foul ooze, and their dress is such
> as is not right to wear in the presence of the gods'
> statues, nor even into any human house.
> I have never seen the tribe that owns this company
> nor know what piece of earth can claim with pride it bore
> such brood, and without hurt and tears for labor given.
>
>   Now after this the master of the house must take
> his own measures: Apollo Loxias, who is very strong
> and heals by divination; reads portentous signs,
> and so clears out the houses others hold as well.

Eumenides 34–63

The scene that the Pythia describes is set within the temple of Apollo. Orestes, as a suppliant of the god, sits on the altar, his status marked by the olive branch wrapped in wool. It is not clear why he would carry the bloody murder-weapon all the way from Argos, except that it would come in handy for fending off the Furies. Also, since blood-guilt was not something that could be washed away with the blood, it would help to make Orestes' case before Apollo all the more urgent if he appeared still holding the murder-weapon and reeking of the crime. As for the Furies, after her initial shock has passed, the Pythia shows herself to be a skilled iconographer. They

143

belong to the rich category of female monsters in Greek popular belief, with closest parallels to two groups in particular, Gorgons and Harpies. The painting she has seen showed the dread, winged Harpies stealing the blind Phineus' food, an episode from the voyage of the Argo (they were captured and punished for this by the sons of Boreas, Zetes and Kalais; cf. Fig. 66). Indeed, the similarities between the Harpies and the Gorgons in Greek art are many, and Aeschylus must have had these in mind in imagining costumes for his Furies. Their evidently obscene dress recalls the fact that painted Gorgons and Harpies often wear extremely short skirts (to facilitate running), sometimes slit all the way up the side. Seen on three-dimensional actors, such an outfit could indeed be shocking.

If a Greek artist of the seventh or sixth century had felt inspired to render this episode, his Furies might well have rivaled Aeschylus' for frightening ugliness. In the event, however, no depictions of the story pre-date the production of the *Oresteia* in 458, and by then a sea-change had come over Attic vase-painters, and even Aeschylus' spectacular *coup de théâtre* could not turn back the clock. Since the invention of the red-figure style, all the female monsters of Greek legend – Gorgons chief among them – had been gradually transformed into beautiful young women, and by the 450s the metamorphosis was just completed. We have here a striking example of the tenacity and independence of artistic convention. On the one hand, the sudden appearance of a group of Attic vases showing Orestes at Delphi and datable to the 450s and 440s is very hard to dissociate from the influence of Aeschylus' *Oresteia*. On the other, not one of these painters was prepared to compromise his esthetic principles by introducing an ugly or monstrous Fury into his scene.

The picture on a krater in San Antonio (Fig. 102) is a good illustration of this, as well as of the painter's determination *not* to reproduce the play as he had seen it on stage. There is no indication of the temple setting, and the pile of uneven rocks on which Orestes kneels could hardly be the altar of the temple. An intriguing suggestion is that this alludes to the "unwrought stones" of the Areopagos in Athens, where the scene of the play will later shift for Orestes' trial. Apollo's laurel branch, aside from being his frequent attribute, could be used in the purification process for Orestes. The same is true of the torch held by the veiled woman at the left, who must be Apollo's sister Artemis. She is, of course, a complete invention of the painter and does not figure in Aeschylus' play at all. We are thus very far from the "theatrical" Oresteia of South Italian red-figure, to which we shall shortly turn.

Attic painters did not, as a rule, ever try to transfer scenes from the tragic stage onto a pot. This is not to say, however, that they were never inspired by their theatre-going experience to add to their repertoire new themes and subjects. Our krater diverges from Aeschylus' play in another fundamental respect: it shows a moment in the story that has passed before the play opens. Orestes' windswept hair and breathless pose imply that he has just

144

Figure 102 Orestes at Delphi. Attic red-figure column-krater, attributed to the Naples Painter. San Antonio Museum of Art 86–134 G (73). Ca. 450.

arrived in Delphi, one step ahead of the Fury in hot pursuit. For a vase-painter this is the meaning of "drama," singling out the moment of greatest action, tension, and suspense. The imaginary dividing-line represented by Apollo's branch, between the frantic chase at the right and the placid divinities at the left, is particularly effective.

In the fourth century, Orestes' plight was a favorite subject of painters all over South Italy, and the imaginative variations with which they depicted it are a tribute both to the vitality of local theatre and to their own originality. The series is extremely varied, and we can only look at a representative sampling.

In Apulian red-figure, where Orestes scenes are most numerous, the story takes on new aspects, sometimes recapturing the active quality of the earliest Attic versions, only now in suitably grand surroundings (Fig. 103). The moment depicted could be considered essentially the same as that on the Attic krater (see Fig. 102): Orestes racing into the Delphic sanctuary, throwing himself upon the Omphalos as Apollo's suppliant with a Fury in close pursuit. The dark gray shading of the Fury's flesh is evidently inspired by Aeschylus' description of them as black; any darker and she would be invisible against the black glaze of the pot. Apollo now intervenes much more actively, as if to signal to the Fury that such creatures are forbidden entry into his sanctuary. At the right is Artemis, not the priestess-like figure of the Attic version, but rather the young huntress, as Greek artists so loved to portray her. The real priestess, meanwhile, who had earlier been depicted as a young woman, has aged here into a new stereotype of the priestess as old woman. A particularly nice touch is the vivid recreation of the Delphic sanctuary, compounded of equal parts authentic detail (the many offerings, from tripod-cauldrons to pieces of armor) and fantasy, in the architectural frame. The whole composition is unthinkable without the painter having witnessed a production of the *Eumenides* – the Pythia fleeing in terror is the best proof of this – yet he has made no attempt to illustrate an actual scene in the play.

A somewhat later Apulian vase, not in such ornate style, perhaps comes closest of any to giving an impression of what the *Eumenides* might have looked like on stage (Fig. 104). The text says several times that Orestes was purified by Apollo with the blood of a pig (284; 450). If this ritual actually took place during the play (silently, so it has left no trace in the text), as has been suggested, then it should have resembled the central group here. Orestes, seated on a simple rectangular altar (the Omphalos is at his back), still clutching the fatal sword, ponders his crime in quiet reverie as Apollo holds the pig over him, as well as the laurel branches probably used in the ritual. The temptation to see this vignette as part of the play is stimulated in

Figure 103 Orestes at Delphi. Apulian red-figure volute-krater attributed to the Black Fury Group. Naples, Museo Nazionale H3249. Ca. 390–370.

146

Figure 104 Purification of Orestes at Delphi. Apulian red-figure bell-krater attributed to the Eumenides Painter, side A. Paris, Louvre K710. Ca. 380–360.

part by the remarkable Aeschylean grouping at the left, two sleeping Furies
roused by the ghost of Klytaimestra (*Eumenides* 94–139). The third Fury
emerging out of the earth can be read as a learned allusion to their chthonic
nature, which becomes particularly relevant in the later scenes of the
Eumenides, when the Furies agree to turn into the benign guardians of the
Attic earth who give the play its title. Artemis would then be the only
noticeable departure from Aeschylus' play, but we have seen how she
became an almost indispensable element in the iconography of the myth.

Lastly, we may turn to yet another school of South Italian red-figure that
favored theatrical scenes, at Paestum (Fig. 105). This version may come
closest to a practise found often in South Italian, to abandon any attempt at
reproducing a dramatic scene, or even combination of scenes, and instead
simply present all the main characters of the drama in an interesting grouping. It has the effect of a particularly artful curtain-call at the end of the play.
Orestes shares center stage with his "co-star" and patron Apollo. Yet each
one's attention is diverted to the side. Orestes is addressed by the goddess
Athena, splendidly dressed and armed, her foot casually propped on a
marble base. Although the setting is nominally Delphi, as indicated by the
huge tripod-cauldron behind Orestes, Athena projects us into the second
half of the play, the trial of Orestes at Athens. Apollo turns briefly to a Fury,
who holds up her snake more like a stage prop than as if she really meant to

147

Figure 105 Orestes at Delphi. Paestan red-figure bell-krater, attributed to Python. London, British Museum 1917.12–10.1. Ca. 330.

use it. The only hint of action in this languorous group comes from a second Fury up above, still wielding live snakes. Finally, busts at the upper left and right must represent Klytaimestra and Pylades. With them we have indeed the entire dramatis personae of the play (and then some), with the exception of the Pythia, whose place is taken by the tripod in which she sat.

SOPHOCLES

Like Aeschylus, Sophocles has left us only seven plays, although we know he produced well over a hundred. Of the seven, three that concern the family of Oedipus – *Oedipus the King*, *Oedipus at Colonus*, *Antigone* – are often thought of as a trilogy, although they are not one in the same sense as the *Oresteia* is, since each was produced years apart. Curiously, the tumultuous events of this Oedipus cycle did not much interest Greek artists. The one episode they consistently favored, the young Oedipus confronting the Theban sphinx, is already long in the past when the first Oedipus play opens. Of Sophocles' other plays, two give us remarkable portraits of familiar epic heroes, probing and frightening psychological studies of noble spirits *in extremis*.

148

DRAMA

Ajax: the suicide of Ajax

As we noted earlier, Pindar often referred to the fate of Ajax, as an example of the treachery that the good-natured suffer at the hands of their fellow men. For Homer, Ajax was the most stout-hearted of the Greek heroes at Troy, the one who could always be counted on for any assignment, no matter how dangerous. His selflessness is epitomized by his rescue of the corpse of Achilles from the fray, a subject beloved of black-figure vase-painters. Ajax rightly felt entitled to the armor of Achilles when it came time to award it, but his claim was challenged by Odysseus. The Greeks agreed to allow each to make his case in a formal speech, to be followed by a public vote, a procedure that was stacked outrageously against Ajax. Odysseus, after all, had the reputation of being the most eloquent and facile speaker of the Greeks, while Ajax's forte was clearly action rather than words. On learning of his defeat, Ajax was driven mad with grief and rage and butchered a flock of sheep, imagining them to be his Greek comrades. When he came to his senses, grief and rage were replaced by a sense of shame so overpowering that he saw no way out but suicide.

We have no idea just how this disturbing tale was narrated in a now lost segment of the Epic Cycle, but it is clear why it appealed to the probing mind and psychological insight of Sophocles. For him, the betrayal of Ajax by his fellow men is compounded by the indifference of the gods, especially Athena, who cold-bloodedly masterminds the whole affair, including the madness of Ajax, for the benefit of her favorite protégé, Odysseus.

The scene of Ajax's suicide is an intensely dramatic one. At a remote location on the shores of Troy, he has determined to plant his sword in the ground and fall upon it. His last words are a soliloquy that only the audience can hear:

> He's firm in the ground, my Slayer. And his cut
> (If I have time even for this reflection)
> Should now be deadliest. For, first, the sword
> Was Hector's gift, a token of guest-friendship,
> And he of all guest-friends my bitterest foe;
> Here, too, it stands, lodged in this hostile ground
> Of Troy, its edge made new with iron-devouring stone.
> And, last, I've propped it, so, with careful handling,
> To help me soon and kindly to my death.
> This preparation I have made. And now,
> Making my invocation, as is right,
> I call first, Zeus, on you. Grant me a little thing:
> Rouse up some messenger for me, to bear
> The news of my disaster first to Teucer,
> So that he first may gently lift me up

149

When I have fallen on this reeking sword.

Ajax 814–28

The prayer goes on to invoke other gods: Hermes, the conductor of souls to the Underworld; Helios, the sun, whose light he sees for the last time; Hades, in whose realm he will shortly be; and the Furies, whose curse Ajax brings down on the two sons of Atreus, Agamemnon and Menelaos, leaders of the Greek army. The prayers, as well as the very manner of death, suggest that Sophocles meant to stage the suicide as a kind of religious ritual, a self-sacrifice.

In the event, it is not Teucer, his brother, who comes upon Ajax's body first, but his wife (actually a prize awarded him from the spoils of war, like Achilles' Briseis), Tekmessa. She forbids the chorus, composed of Ajax's men, to look on the body, but instead uses her own garment, like a shroud, to cover it:

You *must* not see him! I will cover him
With this enfolding garment from all sight.
She removes her own mantle, which should be ample and rectangular,
and covers him

Surely no one who loved him could endure
To see the foam at his nostrils and the spout
Of darkening blood from the wound his own hand made.
Alas, what shall I do? Which of your friends
Will bear you up? Where's Teucer? Oh, may he come in time
To give fit tendance to his fallen brother!
Ajax! To be so great, and suffer this!
Even your enemies, I think, might weep for you.

Ajax 915–24

Ajax's enemies do not weep for him, and instead his unburied body becomes an ugly bone of contention, like that of Polyneikes in the *Antigone*. This last third of the play is surely all Sophocles' invention and is remarkable for its unflattering portrayal of no fewer than three of the great Homeric heroes: Odysseus, Menelaos, and Agamemnon.

The story of Ajax's suicide made a deep impression on Greek artists from an early date, especially the horrific manner in which he accomplished it, which never varies in our literary or visual sources. A fine representative of Early Archaic art is a drinking cup made in Corinth in the early years of the sixth century (Fig. 106). In this version, which must be close to that told in the epic *Aithiopis*, the body is discovered by Ajax's comrades, or, rather, soon after it has been discovered, the chief among them gather to ponder his fate. Thanks to inscriptions, we know who all seven are, and the choice is quite interesting, as is their hierarchical arrangement. Nearest the corpse are the two elderly, white-haired counsellors of the Greek camp, Nestor and Phoinix. They have seen and experienced more than anyone else, and at this

Figure 106 Greek heroes finding the dead Ajax. Middle Corinthian cup attributed to the Cavalcade Painter. Basel, Antikenmuseum (loan). Ca. 580.

unnerving moment the others would turn to them for comfort and advice. Behind these two are, to the right, Agamemnon as commander-in-chief and, to the left, Odysseus. There is no sense of Odysseus as the villain of the piece; he is simply one of the major heroes who is always on hand at key moments. The scene is filled out by three whose relatively junior status is implied by their nudity, in contrast to the long robes of their elders. They include Diomedes, at the left, Teucer, and the Lesser Ajax, son of Oileus, who often fought alongside his more famous namesake. The inclusion of Teucer, in particular, proves that all the names are carefully chosen, or that the painter followed carefully his epic source. Within the conventions of Corinthian vase-painting, the conversational gestures of their outstretched hands make the heroes look oddly detached and pedestrian at this harrowing moment. In a curious way, their loquaciousness seems to trivialize the awful deed, much as the haggling over Ajax's corpse in Sophocles' play saps the emotional and dramatic power of his death. The one element that redeems the Corinthian painter's scene is the magnificent size of the fallen Ajax's body, dwarfing all the others and monumental even in death.

The unforgettable image of Ajax's massive body pierced by a sword turns up throughout Greek art of the sixth century, although nowhere so often as in Corinth. To break out of this schema required the imagination and sensitivity of a great artist like the Athenian Exekias (Fig. 107). It is rare in this early phase of western art that we sense a real sympathy between artist and subject, verging on a feeling of identification. It is equally astonishing that Exekias has captured so much of the ethos of Sophocles' play a full

151

Figure 107 Ajax prepares to fall on his sword. Attic black-figure amphora, by Exekias. Boulogne-sur-Mer, Musée Communal 558. Ca. 530.

century in advance: the loneliness of the solitary act by the barren shore; the methodical behavior of the hero, not at all the actions of a madman; and his troubled demeanor (indicated by lines incised on brow and cheeks), as he broods upon a fate over which he feels he has no control. Much could be said about the masterful composition of the scene: the helmet propped on the big Boeotian shield, giving the impression of a ghostly onlooker (or even Ajax himself, in his former life as the great battle hero); or the palm tree that "wilts in sympathy" (Hurwit 1982). Exekias has created a psychological study that stands virtually alone in Archaic Greek narrative art.

In Attic black-figure it was primarily Exekias who kept alive interest in Ajax by depicting him in a variety of scenes. After about 500, red-figure painters turned increasingly to the hero, perhaps in part because he was now one of the official ten Eponymous Heroes of the state, after the Kleisthenic reorganization of ca. 508. This gradual co-opting of the Salaminian Ajax into an Athenian hero is briefly evident in some of the last words of his farewell speech in Sophocles' play: "O radiance, O my home and hallowed ground of Salamis, and my father's hearth, farewell! And glorious Athens, and my peers and kin" (859–61).

It was usually Ajax's deeds at Troy that these painters now preferred to the scene of his death, with one spectacular exception (Fig. 108). This cup tondo could be an illustration of the moment, quoted above, when Tekmessa

152

covers her husband's corpse, were it not a half century earlier than Sophocles' play. For the first time Ajax has fallen backwards onto the sword. This enables the painter to show us his powerful hairy chest, luxuriant beard, and wildly disheveled hair, perhaps alluding to his earlier madness. His huge size is once again stressed, this time by having the feet project beyond the edge of the circular field. Tekmessa is a conventional female figure for the period, but the garment she unfolds, with its dark patterned border and little weights at the corners, is a nice homely touch. The painter's boldest experiment is his drawing of the sandy and pebbly beach on the Trojan coast. In a period when Greek art shied away from the naturalistic rendering of any landscape elements, this is truly unique.

Knowing the Brygos Painter and his sophisticated interest in complex narratives (cf. Figs. 25–27, by a close associate of the painter), we may not be surprised to find a related subject on the exterior of the cup (Fig. 109). Yet we may still be unprepared for the immensely thoughtful "trilogy" he has created. It is only a pity that the loss of several large fragments prevents a full appreciation of what was once a great masterpiece. Ajax's suicide was, as we have noted, preceded by a vote to award the arms of Achilles, and that vote was in turn preceded by a nasty row between the two main contenders. (The debating match is depicted only once, on a black-figure vase.) These are the

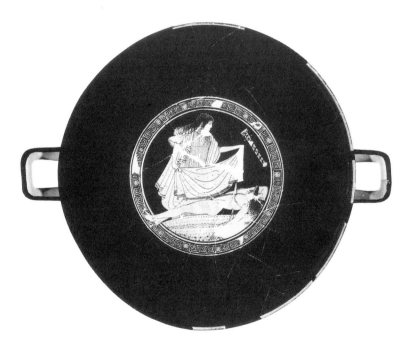

Figure 108 Tekmessa covers the body of Ajax. Attic red-figure cup, attributed to the Brygos Painter, interior. Malibu, J. Paul Getty Museum 86.AE.286. Ca. 490–480.

Figure 109 Agamemnon interrupts a fight among Greek heroes; the vote for the arms of Achilles. Sides A and B of the cup shown in Fig. 108 (p. 153).

stages in the action that the Brygos painter has given us. On one side, two warriors – no doubt Ajax and Odysseus – are restrained from going at each other with drawn swords by several of their comrades. The majestic striding figure in the center, happily well preserved, must be Agamemnon, marked by his scepter and kingly robes. In other mythological contexts, Zeus often occupies this role of mediator. Perhaps we should imagine that Agamemnon is here decreeing the vote that takes place on the reverse.

The voting, with pebbles, is straightforward and democratic (perhaps an echo of the young Athenian democracy): a simple majority wins. Fifteen pebbles are piled at the left edge of the block, fourteen at the right. This calculation has obviously just been made by Ajax, watching from the right handle zone, and he clutches his head with the sudden realization that he has lost. We can see his mind starting to race, filling with confusion and dark thoughts. If Ajax is here, Odysseus must be the figure at the far left, but unfortunately we are deprived of his gesture and expression of triumph. We can say, however, that he was accompanied by Athena, whose feminine drapery and fringed aegis stand out from the crowd. This is the proof that when Sophocles gave Athena the villain's role in his play, he was only following a lead in the epic tradition. The epic will not, of course, actually have placed the goddess in the scene of the vote for the arms; this was rather the contribution of the Athenian vase-painters who, as we have seen, took every opportunity to include their city goddess alongside the heroes she favored.

Trachiniai: the death of Nessos

Another noble and long-suffering Sophoclean wife who finds out how difficult it is being married to a great hero is Deianeira. As a girl she had been married off to Herakles by her father, the Aetolian king Oineus. However, Herakles' heroic career often kept him away from home, and there were other problems besides. Because of an inadvertent murder, Herakles had to leave his native Thebes and settled with his family in the Thessalian town of Trachis. On one of his adventures, in the Peloponnese, he fell in love with a young princess, Iole, and won her from her father, King Eurytos. In a gesture that was probably more thoughtless than malicious, he sent his new bride ahead to Trachis, to be entertained by his wife until such time as he should arrive home. The situation recalls somewhat the arrival of Agamemnon at Mycenae, his concubine Kassandra beside him in the chariot, to the welcome of his wife; but Deianeira is no Klytaimestra, and instead of plotting murder, she can only wring her hands in helpless confusion. She shares her thoughts with the chorus of local women and recalls a fateful incident early in her marriage to Herakles:

> I have had hidden in a copper urn
> for many years the gift of a centaur, long ago.
> While I was still a child, I took it from the wounds
> of the hairy-chested Nessus as he was dying.
> He used to ferry people, for a fee, across
> the deep flood of the Evenus, in his arms
> with no oars to drive him over nor ships' sails.
> I too was carried on his shoulders when my father
> sent me to follow Heracles for the first time
> as his wife. When I was halfway across
> his hands touched me lustfully. I cried out and at once
> the son of Zeus turned around, raised his hands,
> and shot a feathered arrow through his chest; into
> his lungs it hissed. The beast spoke his last words to me
> as he died: "Daughter of old Oeneus,
> if you listen to me, you shall have great profit
> from my ferrying, since you are the last I have brought across.
> If you take in your hands this blood, clotted in
> my wounds, wherever it is black with the bile
> of the Hydra, the monstrous serpent of Lerna, in which
> he dipped his arrows, you will have a charm over

the heart of Heracles, so he will never look
at another woman and love her more than you."
I have thought of this, my friends, for since his death
I have kept it in the house, tightly closed.
I followed all instructions he gave me while he still lived
and dipped this robe in the charm. Now it is all done.

Trachiniai 555–81

Sophocles was surely not the first to tell the story of the death of Nessos, but since all Archaic versions are lost, or merely alluded to in later writers, his is the earliest connected narrative. This makes it very hard to determine which elements might have been added by the playwright. The robe soaked in Nessos' blood, for example, is not mentioned before Sophocles, although it is difficult to imagine that he invented it completely. The motif of Herakles' arrows made more deadly by being dipped in the Hydra's blood is an old one, as we have seen in Stesichoros' poem on Geryon (Chapter 3). Sophocles, however, may well have been the first to make the connection between the killing of Nessos and Herakles' own death, many years later, in the fatal robe unwittingly given him by his wife.

In contrast to literary sources, the iconographic evidence for Herakles and Nessos is abundant throughout the Archaic period, in many parts of the Greek world; but even a glance at the representations is unsettling, for they offer no consensus on one crucial point – the manner of Nessos' death.

Near the beginning of the series is an impressive vase that can lay claim to one of the earliest complex and clearly identifiable mythological narratives in Greek art. It is a big Proto-Attic neck-amphora, datable on style to the second quarter of the seventh century (Figs. 110 and 111). The painter clearly had little experience drawing centaurs. His solution was to render Nessos as a complete, massively proportioned man, then graft on somewhat awkwardly the hindquarters of a horse. He collapses to the ground, fatally wounded by Herakles' sword. The hero strides toward Nessos, but his rear leg is overlapped by his chariot, with Deianeira sitting in the car and watching the encounter. She holds the reins of the four splendid horses. The background of the picture is fairly alive with a bizarre variety of plant and animal life, yet we have no difficulty distinguishing narrative scene from ornamental filler. The composition has a remarkable clarity and specificity, only it has little to do with the events as Deianeira would recount them two centuries later in Sophocles' play. The setting is not a river, for Herakles and his bride are traveling by chariot when accosted by the centaur. If Nessos had taken sexual liberties with Deianeira, there is no indication of that here, and Herakles dispatches him with a sword and not an arrow.

It would be easy to explain this vase away as early and "pre-canonical," in its approach to the myth, as so many Proto-Attic vases are (cf. Fig. 95). But in fact, when Attic black-figure of the sixth century did develop a canonical

Figures 110 and 111 Herakles fights Nessos. Proto-Attic neck-amphora attributed to the Painter of the New York Nessos Amphora (name vase). New York, Metropolitan Museum 11.210.1. Ca. 670–650.

Figures 112 and 113 Herakles killing Nessos. Caeretan black-figure hydria attributed to the Eagle Painter, handle zone. Rome, Villa Giulia. Ca. 520.

Figure 114 Herakles rescuing Deianeira from Nessos. Red-figure cup attributed to Aristophanes. Boston, Museum of Fine Arts 00.345. Ca. 400.

formula for this story, Herakles' weapon is still the sword. The only significant difference from the Proto-Attic amphora is that the chariot is omitted and Deianeira is often perched precariously on Nessos' back, to suggest his sexual offense. There is no trace of the river.

To find a version that comes close to what Sophocles had in mind, we must move outside Greece altogether, to a workshop in Etruria (possibly of East Greek origin) producing the so-called "Caeretan hydriae" (Figs. 112 and 113). Although numbering only a few dozen, all made in the second half of the sixth century, each of these vases is a gem, especially in their refreshing approach to iconography and narrative. The front of this hydria has one of the finest renderings of the blinding of Polyphemos, while the scene that interests us is tucked discreetly under the vertical handle. At last we have a Herakles firing an arrow at Nessos, while Deianeira flees in distress. It is hard to tell if she is more worried about Nessos' advance or Herakles' aim. The painter has cleverly used the natural division of the vase handle to give the proper distance between the archer and his victim. We might even believe he had in mind the setting by the river, when we notice the leafy shrub growing under the side handle, just ahead of Nessos. The little monkey-like creature should not be thought of as an indicator of setting, for such decorative oddities often populate the interstices of these amusing vases.

159

Although Herakles' rescue of his wife from the lascivious centaur appears a handful of times in Attic red-figure, it was clearly a subject for Archaic art much more than Classical. Nor can it be said that the *Trachiniai* had any noticeable impact on the visual tradition. A cup tondo of the last years of the fifth century offers a good example of the artistic spirit of the times, by one of the last red-figure painters who proudly signed his work (Fig. 114), Aristophanes (no relation to the playwright, that we know of). Herakles has been transformed into the young beardless hero that Classical art preferred, and he now wields his club. If the painter knew the story of the blood of Nessos, it was certainly far from his mind when he painted the scene. After several generations of big battle scenes between Greeks and centaurs, in sculpture as well as painting, artists have perfected the Classical centaur, with human and equine elements merging seamlessly. There is even a certain eroticism about Nessos' bestiality and brute strength as he lifts Deianeira effortlessly off the ground. She is, like almost all women in vase-painting of this period, elegantly dressed and coiffed, not at all disheveled in her ordeal. The cup is one of an identical pair made by the potter Erginos and decorated by Aristophanes, although they signed only one. The exteriors of both cups are filled with the Thessalian Centauromachy, which actually did not involve either Nessos or Herakles, but other heroes and other centaurs.

EURIPIDES

If we are to judge by the number of surviving plays (nineteen, as against seven each of Aeschylus and Sophocles), as well as ceramic representations, then Euripides must be considered the most popular and most often produced tragic playwright of antiquity. His enormous success in the western Greek colonies, even in his own lifetime, is attested by a famous anecdote, that the Athenian soldiers captured in the disaster at Syracuse in 413 were in some instances able to win their freedom by reciting favorite passages from Euripides (Plutarch, *Life of Nikias* 29.3).

The playwright drew his material from a wide range of sources, but almost exclusively from the epic tradition and the genealogies of the heroic age, whether in Thebes, Corinth, Thessaly, or his native Athens. In every instance, however, figures who seem rather two-dimensional in the epic – and this is especially true of female characters – come alive on the Euripidean stage as fascinating psychological studies. Through this dramatic technique, the playwright was able to make the heroic tales of a bygone era relevant to the most topical issues of contemporary Athens, whether it be the havoc wrought by war, the role of traditional religion in a "modern" world, or the situation of women in a strongly patriarchal society.

Trojan Women: the fall of Troy

Perhaps half of Euripides' prolific output was produced during the long years of the Peloponnesian War (431–404). Whereas an earlier generation of Athenians had proudly drawn parallels between the Trojan War and the Persian Wars, both Greek victories over eastern "barbarians," when Euripides looked for parallels between the epic struggle and the one raging around him, he saw only the darker side: the suffering of women and children, the moral degradation brought on by prolonged warfare.

A poet of the Epic Cycle had composed a lengthy work on the *Iliupersis*, or sack of Troy, that one long night when the Greek army, finally gaining access to Priam's city by the ruse of the Trojan Horse, vented the rage of ten years' frustrating siege. The catalog of atrocities committed that night was long – too long for Euripides to cram them all into a single play. As it is, the play may seem relentlessly bleak and at times threatens to degenerate into a grisly game of "Can you top this?" as each new horror that is related overshadows the one before. The one element that, in this context, provides almost comic relief is the encounter of Menelaos and his unfaithful wife Helen, for whom the war was fought. She is defiant, still unrepentant (so different from the self-lacerating Helen of the *Iliad*), and eventually quiets Menelaos' wrath with her still formidable sexual charms.

The figure who bears the brunt of the suffering is Hecuba, noble matriarch of the Trojan royal family, who must witness the murder or enslavement of all her nearest and dearest. In one of her laments she describes the reversal of fortune that has turned her from the most fortunate of women to the most miserable:

> I was a princess, who was once a prince's bride,
> mother by him of sons pre-eminent, beyond
> the mere numbers of them, lords of the Phrygian domain,
> such sons for pride to point to as no woman of Troy,
> no Hellene, none in the outlander's wide world might match.
> And then I saw them fall before the spears of Greece,
> and cut this hair for them, and laid it on their graves.
> I mourned their father, Priam. None told me the tale
> of his death. I saw it, with these eyes. I stood to watch
> his throat cut, next the altar of the protecting god.
> I saw my city taken. And the girls I nursed,
> choice flowers to wear the pride of any husband's eyes,
> matured to be dragged by hands of strangers from my arms.
> There is no hope left that they will ever see me more,
> no hope that I shall ever look on them again.
> There is one more stone to key this arch of wretchedness:
> I must be carried away to Hellas now, an old

161

slave woman, where all those tasks that wrack old age shall be
given me by my masters. I must work the bolt
that bars their doorway, I whose son was Hector once;
or bake their bread; lay down these withered limbs to sleep
on the bare ground, whose bed was royal once; abuse
this skin once delicate the slattern's way, exposed
through robes whose rags will mock my luxury of long since.
Unhappy, O unhappy. And all this came to pass
and shall be, for the way one woman chose a man.
Cassandra, O Daughter, whose excitements were the god's,
you have paid for your consecration now; at what a price!
And you, my poor Polyxena, where are you now?
Not here, nor any boy or girl of mine, who were
so many once, is near me in my unhappiness.

Trojan Women 474–504

Of her daughters, she singles out two whose fates will be especially cruel.
Kassandra, already half-mad from the prophetic powers Apollo had given
her, will be raped by a Greek hero, the Lesser Ajax, before being carried off
to Greece (and her own death) by Agamemnon (cf. Fig. 90). Polyxena will
be slaughtered like a sacrificial offering at the tomb of Achilles. And this is
not all. The Trojans' brightest hope for the next generation is little Astyanax,
son of Hektor and Andromache. His mother will go to Greece as a slave,
like the others, but the boy cannot be allowed to live (Euripides puts the
blame on Odysseus, l. 721). In a grim symmetry, Neoptolemos, the young
son of Achilles who joined the war only at the end, will kill the son of
Hektor by hurling him from the battlements of Troy.

It is little wonder that Archaic Greek artists, with their taste for action and
violence, made the sack of Troy one of their favorite subjects from an early
date; but from the point of view of narrative, the story presented a special
challenge, since it comprised so many diverse episodes that all happened
more or less at once. It was an embarrassment of riches. One possibility was
to focus on a single incident – the rape of Kassandra, say, or the death of
Priam – and many artists did just that; but for those who felt inspired to try
to capture the panorama of destruction, it required an ingenuity that tested
the limits of early Greek narrative art.

Our perception of the narrative sophistication of seventh-century Greek
artists was radically altered some thirty years ago, with the discovery on the
island of Mykonos of a huge clay pithos (storage-jar) decorated in low relief
(Fig. 115). The large square panel on the neck presents by far the most
imaginative preserved rendering of the Trojan Horse. While Trojan soldiers
climb and poke about the strange contraption on wheels, the Greeks concealed inside peer out of little "windows," as if sitting in an airplane. After
much deliberation, and against the advice of some, the Trojans will wheel the

creature through the gates of the city, inviting their own destruction. This is the subject of the body of the vase, ingeniously divided into individual square panels, like the metopes of a Doric temple, in several superimposed friezes. In one respect the artist's conception has much in common with Euripides: he sees the devastation mainly from the viewpoint of the Trojan women. Most of the poses and gestures are too generalized to allow us to put a name on individual figures. In one instance, where we see a man swinging a child as a woman implores him, we are surely entitled to think of Neoptolemos with Andromache and Astyanax. Adjacent to this group is another woman clutching a child to protect it from a Greek sword, reminding us that Astyanax was not the only Trojan child to die that night. The metope composition is obviously well suited to the story of the Iliupersis, yet, curiously, it was never adapted to the painted surface of later vases.

Instead, Attic black-figure painters met the challenge of the Iliupersis by experimenting with different ways of merging several episodes into a coherent composition. One of the earliest and most successful was by Lydos (Fig. 116). The other side of this amphora shows Achilles ambushing the

Figure 115 The Trojan Horse (neck) and the sack of Troy (body). Relief pithos. Mykonos, Museum. Ca. 675.

Figure 116 Sack of Troy: the deaths of Priam and Astyanax. Attic black-figure amphora, attributed to Lydos. Berlin, Pergamon Museum 1685. Ca. 550–540.

young Trojan prince Troilos, whose death, it was prophesied, was a precondition for the Greeks' taking of Troy. There is thus a subtle thematic link between the two sides of the vase, surprising at this early date. The reverse panel manages to fit eight figures into the limited trapezoidal space, yet so clearly and symmetrically articulated that each enjoys his full impact on the viewer. The focus is on the confrontation of Priam and his killer, Neoptolemos. All sources (including Euripides) agree that the defenseless old king was slain at an altar, an act of profound impiety and brutality. Although many scenes of this period show Priam lying dead across the altar, here the drama is heightened by showing an earlier moment: the king reaching out his hand to touch Neoptolemos' chin, the traditional gesture of supplication. As we noted in a scene of the raging Achilles (see Fig. 16), the big helmet is used effectively to dehumanize the assailant, precluding any expression or reaction. In his right hand, Neoptolemos swings the limp body of Astyanax, as if he were going to use it as a weapon. A grotesque thought: to wield the child against his own grandfather.

The two women who watch the scene from the right are not labeled, but we may reasonably assume them to be Hecuba and Andromache, the one pleading for her husband's life, the other for her son's. They are balanced compositionally at the left by the pair of Helen and Menelaos. His hand disappears behind her back as he evidently grasps her garment, brandishing a sword in the other hand. His first intention, we are told, was to send Helen straight to her death, until a glimpse of her bared breast made his resolve crumble. The last figure in the scene is that of a dead Trojan stretched out behind the altar. He could be another of the many sons of Priam whom

164

Hecuba had to watch cut down. His position makes us flash back to Hektor, dragged by Achilles' chariot or lying beneath Achilles' couch (see Figs. 16 and 17; 24 and 25). Although Hektor is long dead by now, in a way his spirit is present as we witness the demise of his whole family.

The fascination with the horrors of war reached something of a crescendo among red-figure painters of the generation ca. 500–480. It has been argued that their increasingly graphic depictions of the sack of Troy were in some way fueled by exultation at the defeat of the Persians in 490 and again in 480/79. This is also, as we have seen, the period of some of the most complex and thoughtful *Iliad* scenes (e.g. Figs. 4–6), so it comes as no surprise that the same artists lavished equal care on rendering the war's climactic moments. Cups were often the favored medium for these ambitious narratives, but the Kleophrades Painter chose the somewhat unlikely surface of a hydria's shoulder to unroll one of the most spectacular of all Iliupersis scenes (Fig. 117).

Through the deliberate crowding and overlapping of figures, a sense of the tumult and confusion is made palpable. Only after this initial sensation do our eyes adjust and we discern two principal groups adjacent to one another in the middle of the scene and various subsidiary figures filling out the sides. One group again shows the deaths of Priam and Astyanax, which by now had come to symbolize most immediately the whole story. This is perhaps the most pitiable Priam of them all, feebly covering his head as Neoptolemos prepares to bring down the fatal blow. The lifeless body of Astyanax lies in Priam's lap. Like Lydos, the painter has reversed the traditional order and placed Astyanax's death before Priam's, to heighten the pathos. We notice immediately how the red-figure technique allowed a far more effective display of blood than black-figure.

The second major group is devoted to the rape of Kassandra, who had sought refuge at the Palladion, an ancient statue of Athena in Troy. In an age when the conventions of Greek art still imposed an almost total ban on depictions of the nude female figure, Kassandra's frontal nudity is both shocking and disturbingly erotic. The background of both groups is filled with dead Trojan warriors and mourning Trojan women.

The cumulative effect of these two acts of brutality is indeed sobering, but as our eye moves out from the center, a ray or two of hope appear. Just behind Neoptolemos, a woman wielding a large pestle goes at a Greek who kneels and brandishes a sword. The woman has been thought to be Andromache, or possibly Polyxena. In either case, her heroic resistance will ultimately be in vain, although just at the moment she seems to have the upper hand. She makes a noble contrast to the passivity of the women who sit helplessly by and prefigures the determination of the royal Trojan women as Euripides will portray them. Further to the right, the frieze ends with an episode of a very different nature: two young warriors rescuing an elderly woman from the fray. She is Aithra, the mother of Theseus, who in old age had somehow ended up in Troy as a handmaiden of Helen (*Iliad* 3.144). The youths are her grandsons, Demophon and Akamas, who will bring her home to Athens. Homer barely knows of these two sons of Theseus, and we may have the feeling that fifth-century Athenians, distressed that their heroic ancestors played so little role in the *Iliad*, have inserted them in an effort to enhance the Athenian participation at Troy.

At the extreme left, the Trojan hero Aeneas carries his aged father Anchises to safety, and his young son Askanios flees alongside. As every Roman knew, Aeneas would make his way to Italy, and out of the ashes of Troy would rise a new race, but that was not the Kleophrades Painter's concern. Rather, he wanted to frame the worst horrors of the war with two acts of *pietas*, to suggest how warfare may bring out the best, as well as the worst, in the human character. The painter could well afford this half-way optimistic vision, for he was living in a proud young democracy that, against

Figure 117 Sack of Troy: counterclockwise, Aeneas rescuing Anchises, rape of Kassandra; deaths of Priam and Astyanax; Andromache (?) fending off a Greek; rescue of Aithra. Attic red-figure hydria, attributed to the Kleophrades Painter. Naples, Museo Nazionale 2422. Ca. 490–480. After A. Furtwängler and K. Reichhold, *Griechische Vasenmalerei* I (Munich, 1904) pl. 34.

kept coming out the victor. Euripides, seventy years later, had no
‸nism, as he watched his city first brutalize its own allies, then
⌐ strife that invited destruction at the hands of Sparta.

in Tauris: Orestes and Iphigenia

⌐m the Trojan Cycle, Euripides seems to have
pursuing the generation after the war itself,
…ple, the later fortunes of the children of Agamemnon.
…genia, his eldest daughter, had already been featured in Euripides'
dramatization of that tragic episode at Aulis, when Agamemnon was compelled to sacrifice his own daughter so that the Greek army might have
favorable winds to sail for Troy.

Later the playwright returned to Iphigenia, since, like most Greek
audiences, he found the sacrifice of Iphigenia unbearably cruel. Instead, he
chose to follow an alternate ending of the story, according to which the
goddess Artemis, who had demanded the sacrifice in the first place, substituted a deer for the young girl at the last minute. Iphigenia was whisked off
to a remote spot on the Black Sea, to serve as priestess of Artemis. Under
orders from the local king, a caricatured barbarian named Thoas, she is to
sacrifice to the goddess any Greek who fetches up on the shores of Tauris.
The Greek who appears is none other than her brother Orestes.

The play is not a conventional tragedy, since it will have a happy ending,
with Orestes and Iphigenia's escape from Tauris and return to Greece; but it
does have considerable suspense, as the brother and sister must outwit the
king to make good their escape. The plot also gave Euripides an opportunity
to contrive a clever recognition scene. Orestes, after all, was no more than a
baby when Iphigenia was "sacrificed," so neither would know the other's
identity. Iphigenia has written a letter to her family back in Greece, explaining her situation, but how to get the letter to them? Since Orestes is, as
always, accompanied by Pylades, she makes a deal with the two strangers,
that she will spare the life of one, on condition that he deliver the letter:

> Precede me into the temple and be ready.
> *The Attendants enter the temple*
> Here is my letter, safe within these folds.
> But I have wondered. A man who has been in danger
> When he comes out of it forgets his fears,
> And sometimes he forgets his promises.
> Might it not happen that your friend, intent
> Upon his own concerns again, forget
> How very much this letter means to me?

Orestes. And what would you suggest, to ease your mind?

Iphigenia. His solemn vow to take this where I say.

Orestes. And will you make a vow balancing his?

Iphigenia. To do what, or undo what?

Orestes.   To make sure
He be allowed to leave this deathly place.
                              Iphigenia in Tauris 725–39

After much discussion of what would happen if the letter were to be lost in a shipwreck, it is agreed that Pylades should memorize its contents:

Pylades. That is a surer way, for both of us.
So whom am I to find for you in Argos?
What shall I say to him?

Iphigenia.   Say this to him.
Say to Orestes, son of Agamemnon,
"A greeting comes from one you think is dead."
Tell him, "Your sister is not dead at Aulis
But is alive."

Orestes.   Alive? Iphigenia?
Oh, no! Unless the dead come back again!

Iphigenia. You are looking at her now, for I am she.
But let me finish what I ask of him.
"O brother, come and save me from a life
As priestess in a loathsome ritual –
Save me from dying in this lonely land."

Orestes. Where am I, Pylades? What am I hearing?

Iphigenia. "Lest memory of me should always haunt you."
The name, you must repeat it, is Orestes.

Orestes. I hear a God!

Iphigenia.   You hear only a woman.

Orestes. I hear a woman – and I hear a God!
Let me hear more! I hear a miracle!

Iphigenia. Then tell him, "Artemis put out Her hand
And spared my life at Aulis, leaving a deer
To bleed instead." And tell him this, "My father,
Not looking when he struck, believed me dead.
Artemis brought me here." The letter ends.
                              Iphigenia in Tauris 766–87

Figures 118 and 119 Iphigenia in Tauris. Attic red-figure calyx-krater attributed to the Iphigeneia Painter (name vase). Ferrara, Museo Archeologico Nazionale T1145. Ca. 380.

Figure 120 Iphigenia in Tauris. Above handle of the calyx-krater shown in Fig. 118 (p. 169).

The joyful reunion of siblings quickly follows.

A late Athenian red-figure painter, who may have seen a revival of Euripides' play in the 380s, has given us our fullest version of the principal characters and the recognition scene (Figs. 118–120). At the very center of the picture is the shrine of Artemis (hardly a temple), in which the primitive cult statue of the goddess stands (see Fig. 118). Iphigenia, resting her elbow casually on the structure, dwarfs it, as she does the two nearly nude figures of Orestes and Pylades below her. There is no doubt that she is the play's title character. She hands the letter to Pylades, who will in turn deliver it to Orestes. This much is the core of the narrative, but the painter, like so many of his contemporaries in South Italy, does not stop there. He gives us a splendid depiction of King Thoas, in his barbarian costume, fanned by an attendant (see Fig. 120), as well as a female attendant of Iphigenia who could stand for the chorus of local women. A woman watching from the upper left may be Artemis herself (see Fig. 119), who does not have a speaking role in the play (it is rather Athena, the *dea ex machina*, who appears at the end to give Orestes and Iphigenia instructions), but in a sense presides over it. It has been suggested that the painter not only gives us the whole cast of the play, but deliberately alludes to other scenes, both earlier and later than the recognition. For example, the rocks by which Orestes and Pylades sit recall their first arrival at the Taurian shore and capture by the herdsman of Thoas, whom we glimpse above the left handle, a youth in barbarian costume (see Fig. 119). The offerings carried by Iphigenia's attendant could look ahead to the scene when Iphigenia, under the pretext of carrying the statue of Artemis in procession to the shore, actually steals it for the return to Greece. We would then have a kind of visual digest of the whole play, nevertheless focused on the pivotal scene which marks both the mid-point and the turning-point of the action.

Bacchae: the death of Pentheus

Late in life, Euripides was invited to the Macedonian court and there produced one of his most beautiful and disturbing plays, the *Bacchae*. For the subject he reached back to the saga of the Theban royal house, which was second only to the Trojan Cycle as the favored source for tragic material; but, as in almost all his plays, Euripides succeeded in making the ancient legend pertinent to his audience by offering a cautionary tale that would have spoken directly to them. Pentheus, the arrogant young king of Thebes, has learned that a new god from the east, Dionysos, has won the hearts of his subjects, especially the women, who worship him in mountain rituals. They call themselves maenads, or bacchai, after the cry with which they invoke the god. Pentheus dismisses the superstition, until a remarkable stranger – the god in disguise – piques his curiosity to see the secret rites. Dionysos manipulates the prudish king, dressing him up in women's clothes (the better to spy on the maenads), all the while planning an exquisite punishment for him. As a messenger recounts the grisly scene, the maenads, led by Pentheus' own mother, Agave, first cornered the hapless youth up a tree:

> Then Agave cried out: "Maenads, make a circle
> about the trunk and grip it with your hands.
> Unless we take this climbing beast, he will reveal
> the secrets of the god." With that, thousands of hands
> tore the fir tree from the earth, and down, down
> from his high perch fell Pentheus, tumbling
> to the ground, sobbing and screaming as he fell,
> for he knew his end was near. His own mother,
> like a priestess with her victim, fell upon him
> first. But snatching off his wig and snood
> so she would recognize his face, he touched her cheeks,
> screaming, "No, no, Mother! I am Pentheus,
> your own son, the child you bore to Echion!
> Pity me, spare me, Mother! I have done a wrong,
> but do not kill your own son for my offense."
> But she was foaming at the mouth, and her crazed eyes
> rolling with frenzy. She was mad, stark mad,
> possessed by Bacchus. Ignoring his cries of pity,
> she seized his left arm at the wrist; then, planting

her foot upon his chest, she pulled, wrenching away
the arm at the shoulder – not by her own strength,
for the god had put inhuman power in her hands.
Ino, meanwhile, on the other side, was scratching off
his flesh. Then Autonoë and the whole horde
of Bacchae swarmed upon him. Shouts everywhere,
he screaming with what little breath was left,
they shrieking in triumph. One tore off an arm,
another a foot still warm in its shoe. His ribs
were clawed clean of flesh and every hand
was smeared with blood as they played ball with scraps
of Pentheus' body.

Bacchae 1106–37

The maenads use no weapons against their victim, only bare hands and the strength the god has breathed into them. It was part of their rites to tear live animals apart, and in their frenzy they mistake Pentheus for a lion. In the harrowing final scene of the play, Agave enters with the head of her son impaled on a thyrsos (fennel stalk), still believing it to be a lion's, until she returns to her senses.

A full century earlier than Euripides' play, the scene of the death of Pentheus had entered the repertoire of Attic red-figure, in a masterful rendering by Euphronios (Figs. 121 and 122). Unfortunately, only about half the scene on this remarkable vase, a wine-cooler (psykter), survives, but enough to make a powerful impression. Down to the last detail it could be an illustration of the Euripidean passage. Pentheus is already dead, but the maenads' fury has not abated as they continue to dismember him. Two have got hold of the upper part of his body, from the head down to the lower chest, now a mass of blood. A streak of blood across Pentheus' closed eye suggests that it has been torn out as well. The maenad at left grips the shoulder and upper arm with both her hands, clearly getting ready to wrest the arm from its socket. The other has got hold of Pentheus' other arm and in her outstretched left hand, now lost, may have held either Pentheus' leg or a thyrsos, like her companion at the left. At any rate, another, non-joining, fragment (see Fig. 122) includes a leg held by another maenad, who brandishes it as if it had just been torn from the body. The only slight discrepancy from Euripides is in the name Galene (literally "calm"!) beside the woman holding Pentheus' torso from the left, where we might have expected Agave or her sister Ino.

Sometime about 480, Aeschylus produced a *Pentheus* that could have inspired the painter Douris to the finest extant version of the death of Pentheus (Figs. 123–125). The cup is much more than an illustration of that event, however. It is a celebration of the god Dionysos and his cult, as is Euripides' play, on a vessel made for the enjoyment of Dionysos' gift of

172

Figure 121 The death of Pentheus. Fragments of Attic red-figure psykter, attributed to Euphronios. Boston, Museum of Fine Arts 10.221. Ca. 510.

Figure 122 Maenad brandishes leg of Pentheus. Additional fragments of the psykter shown in Fig. 121 (above).

Figure 123 Maenad. Attic red-figure cup, attributed to Douris, interior. Formerly Toronto, Borowski Collection. Ca. 480. Courtesy *LIMC*.

Figure 124 Death of Pentheus: Dionysos, maenads and dismembered Pentheus. Attic red-figure cup, attributed to Douris. Side A of the cup shown in Fig. 123 (above). Courtesy *LIMC*.

Figure 125 Death of Pentheus: Dionysos, maenads and dismembered Pentheus. Attic red-figure cup, attributed to Douris. Side B of the cup shown in Fig. 123 (p. 174). Courtesy *LIMC*.

wine. We have become accustomed to finding uncommonly complex narratives on red-figure cups of this period, and this is no exception. In fact, it adds a new element of sophistication, for if the three scenes are read in the correct order, they offer a sequence of tension and resolution very much akin to the experience of the theatre audience on whom the terrible denouement dawns only gradually. We start in the tondo (see Fig. 123), where a solitary maenad dances as she holds her thyrsos and a tame-looking baby leopard by the tail. Although this is surely not how felines prefer to be held, this one does not seem to mind. The maenad's attention has been caught by something, and so we too turn the cup over expectantly.

The god Dionysos himself occupies the center of one side (see Fig. 124), holding his wine in a capacious kantharos and an ivy branch in his upraised hand. He turns to listen to the music of a piping satyr, but otherwise looks relaxed and well pleased. The maenads seem at first to be swaying to the music, until we notice that the objects they hold are not the usual small animals, but human body-parts, thighs and a leg with bone protruding. There is something further unsettling in the frontal faces of two of the maenads, a device so rare in Attic vase-painting that it usually suggests an extraordinary mental state.

By now we are prepared for the worst, but the full horror is only revealed when we turn to the other side (see Fig. 125) and see Pentheus' head and torso, severed at the waist, guts spilling out. Two maenads work him over, as meticulous as surgeons (scratching off his flesh, as Euripides' messenger

175

Figure 126 Maenads attacking Pentheus. Apulian red-figure dish attributed to the Group of Oxford G269. Ruvo, Jatta Collection 1617. Ca. 360–350.

describes), while the only one looking truly frenzied is the more mature woman twisting the victim's cloak. She has been plausibly identified as Agave. The satyr at the right gives us a third frontal face, to heighten the excitement and the horror.

In the remainder of the fifth century, depictions of the episode are rare, but it is likely that Euripides' play revived interest, since we find it often on fourth-century South Italian vases. A fine Attic version of about 420, too fragmentary to illustrate here, introduces a new interpretation, later adopted in Magna Graecia, that speaks volumes about the different ethos of Archaic and Classical art. The moment depicted is now an earlier one, so that Pentheus is still intact and struggling vainly for survival. A fine example of this type is an Apulian cup (Fig. 126), whose other side, like the Douris cup (see Fig. 124), shows Dionysos relaxing with his entourage. Pentheus makes a splendid heroic figure, his cloak billowing out behind him and brandishing a sword. If we did not know the outcome of the story, we might well think he will fend off the attack of these four rather delicate-looking females. The sword wielded by one of the maenads, a real violation of the spirit of Euripides' play, shows that the painters were not concerned with fidelity to a literary source. The gruesome spectacle of the dismembered Pentheus was clearly more than the refined tastes of Late Classical art could endure. By recasting the story in this way, however, artists reduced it to a conventional battle-scene, with none of the Dionysian fury that shakes anyone who has seen Euripides' *Bacchae* on the stage.

Medea: the killing of the children and the escape from Corinth

The horror of killing one's own blood relative, under whatever circumstances, must have exercised an endless fascination for Greek audiences.

Although many permutations of the motif occur in Greek myth – sons killing fathers, brother against brother – there seems to be a particular interest in the mutually destructive relationship of mothers and sons. We saw it in Orestes' murder of his mother Klytaimestra, then, in a reversal (and in an utterly different situation), Agave killing her son Pentheus. A second Euripidean drama builds to a similarly terrifying climax, in which a mother kills her two sons, not in ignorance or frenzy, but as a coldly calculated act of revenge on their father.

Jason's success in his quest for the Golden Fleece, as we have seen (Chapter 3), was dependent on the help of Medea, whose consuming love for him drove her to put her magic arts at his service, even if this meant betraying her own family. In so doing, she tied her own fortunes inextricably to those of Jason and had no choice but to accompany him back to Greece as his wife. Once they are back in "civilization," Euripides gives us to understand, the romantic idyll starts to crumble. For Medea, as a foreign woman, is not easily accepted by the Greek community (in Corinth, where the couple has settled), and Jason cannot understand why his wife is not eternally grateful for her "rescue" from the barbarian east. The crisis comes when Jason proposes to marry the daughter of the local king, a politically advantageous move. Medea's reaction to being pushed aside in favor of a younger woman is very different from the hapless Deianeira's, although, by a curious twist, the results bear a striking similarity in one respect; for Medea too has a magic potion which, when applied to a garment, turns it into a death-trap. She sends the princess the fatal robe as a gift, and both the girl and her father are consumed in the conflagration.

This is only the start of Medea's vengeance. On hearing what has happened at the palace, Jason, who has never really understood his wife, jumps to all the wrong conclusions:

> *Jason.* You women, standing close in front of this dwelling,
> Is she, Medea, she who did this dreadful deed,
> Still in the house, or has she run away in flight?
> For she will have to hide herself beneath the earth,
> Or raise herself on wings into the height of air,
> If she wishes to escape the royal vengeance.
> Does she imagine that, having killed our rulers,
> She will herself escape uninjured from this house?
> But I am thinking not so much of her as for
> The children – her the king's friends will make to suffer
> For what she did. So I have come to save the lives
> Of my boys, in case the royal house should harm them
> While taking vengeance for their mother's wicked deed.
>
> *Chorus.* O Jason, if you but knew how deeply you are
> involved in sorrow, you would not have spoken so.

Jason. What is it? That she is planning to kill me also?

Chorus. Your children are dead, and by their own mother's hand.

Jason. What! That is it? O woman, you have destroyed me!

Chorus. You must make up your mind your children are no more.

Jason. Where did she kill them? Was it here or in the house?

Chorus. Open the gates and there you will see them murdered.

Jason. Quick as you can unlock the doors, men, and undo
The fastenings and let me see this double evil,
My children dead and her – Oh her I will repay.

*His attendants rush to the door. Medea appears above the house in
a chariot drawn by dragons. She has the dead bodies
of the children with her*

Medea. Why do you batter these gates and try to unbar them,
Seeking the corpses and for me who did the deed?
You may cease your trouble, and, if you have need of me,
Speak, if you wish. You will never touch me with your hand,
Such a chariot has Helius, my father's father,
Given me to defend me from my enemies.

Jason. You hateful thing, you woman most utterly loathed
By the gods and me and by all the race of mankind,
You who have had the heart to raise a sword against
Your children, you, their mother, and left me childless –
You have done this, and do you still look at the sun
And at the earth, after these most fearful doings?

Medea 1293–328

Jason's cry that Medea would have to "raise herself on wings" to escape punishment is, of course, prophetic, since this is just what she does. The chariot drawn by winged dragons is a gift from her grandfather, the sun god, and is the perfect getaway car for a witch who had earlier demonstrated her ability to deal with a dragon (see Fig. 66). The chariot will carry her to Athens, where King Aegeus, appearing unexpectedly in Corinth earlier in the play, had offered her refuge, should she ever need to get out of Corinth.

Neither Medea's killing of her children nor her escape from Corinth was a subject for Greek art down through the fifth century. This is odd, since an earlier crime of Medea's – persuading the daughters of Pelias to chop up their father with a false promise of rejuvenating him – had been a favorite subject in Attic vase-painting since the late sixth century. One wonders just how much of the later story, including the dragon chariot, might have been original with Euripides, whose play was produced in 431. If the play did not make an impression on Athenian painters of the late fifth century, it certainly did on South Italian artists who saw road-company productions of it throughout the colonies of Magna Graecia.

No painter captured both the excitement and the sobering effect of this final scene of the play as brilliantly as a Lucanian master of the very end of the fifth century (Fig. 127). Medea, dressed in the finest "barbarian" theatre costume, is already aloft. Her twin dragons, although splendid beasts, are, surprisingly, without wings. Perhaps they do not need them, for the car is magically transported in a huge nimbus provided by the sun god. We may be so dazzled by this that only afterwards do we notice the gruesome spectacle of the two slaughtered boys stretched out limply on a bloody altar. An elderly woman and man, representing two stock characters of Attic tragedy, nurse and paidagogos, recoil in horror. The pitiful figure of Jason at the bottom left is a stroke of genius, a portrait of unalloyed suffering and humiliation. The garment slipping to his waist makes him look especially puny, and his ravaged face is contorted in grief. The only addition to Euripides' play that the painter has allowed himself is the pair of Furies watching from above, and here he is perfectly justified. Euripides' ending is almost perverse in its celebration of Medea's triumph, while the painter reminds us that no shedding of kindred blood goes unpunished by the Furies. Thus his Medea does not escape scot-free, and we are invited to think beyond the boundaries of the play. A final indication of the painter's thoughtfulness and originality is evident in his defying the conventions of his art and giving us truly ugly and grotesque Furies. While the Furies who pursue Orestes had regularly been beautified in both Attic and South Italian (see e.g. Figs. 102 and 105), here is finally a pair we could imagine on the Aeschylean stage.

To appreciate the diversity of the South Italian schools of red-figure, we may consider a Campanian example and end with one from the most prolific school, in Apulia. The Campanian amphora (Fig. 128) is one of several that were clearly inspired by Euripides' play and yet illustrate a moment that no one could have seen, the killing of Medea's children. That took place inside the palace, like most murders in Attic tragedy, out of sight of the audience. Early on, however, as we saw on the Lucanian krater, artists hit on the idea that the two boys should have been slain at (or on) an altar. It is hard to say whether this was inspired by an alternate literary version of the myth or perhaps by an artistic contamination with other scenes of children slaughtered at an altar (e.g. Astyanax, see Fig. 117). The Campanian painter's scene thus comes from his own imagination, although it seems to presuppose a knowledge of the Euripidean scene, in which we hear the pleas for mercy and help of first the one son, then the other. Here one boy lies already dead on the altar, while Medea grabs the other brusquely by the hair as he is about to flee. She manages at the same time to hold onto her sword and is encumbered by the scabbard in her other hand. The old paidagogos, a family

179

Figure 127 Medea's escape from Corinth. Lucanian calyx-krater, near the Policoro Painter. Cleveland Museum of Art 91.1 (Leonard C. Hanna, Jr. Fund). Ca. 400.

Figure 128 Medea killing her children. Campanian amphora attributed to the Painter of British Museum F223. Paris, Cabinet des Médailles 876. Ca. 350–320.

retainer and companion of the two boys, watches from behind a sloping ground line.

Until the recent appearance of the Lucanian krater (see Fig. 127), the most impressive artistic vision of the Medea story was that on an Apulian krater in Munich, often known simply as *the* Medea vase (Fig. 129). In striking contrast to the Lucanian painter's fidelity to both the letter and the spirit of Euripides' play, this artist either preferred to follow another dramatic treatment of the same events, one that in the literary tradition has been completely overshadowed by Euripides' masterpiece, or else reshaped the basic plot with a substantial admixture of his own imagination.

Apart from questions of content, the Apulian painter's approach to narrative is totally different, combining at least three discrete scenes into one multi-level composition, with subsidiary figures who may allude to several more. The Apulian love of grandiose architecture is reflected in the handsome six-columned Ionic structure that dominates the scene, representing the palace of King Kreon of Corinth. Inside it we see the final agonies of the princess, caused not by a robe, but some kind of hat or veil. Her father looks suitably distraught, but does not seem in danger of being caught up in his daughter's fate, as in Euripides. Instead, the girl's brother comes to her rescue, but too late. Below, Medea is about to stab one of her sons on an altar, as Jason looks on helplessly. They are separated by the serpent chariot, which waits quietly for Medea and blocks Jason's access to his children. In this version, only one of the children dies, the other led away to safety by a young man while Medea is busy with the killing.

A further variant is that the chariot comes complete with a driver, a young man with snakes in his hair and torches in his hands, labelled "Oistros" (Gadfly). This personification, one of several in South Italian vase-painting representing different states of madness, seems to imply that Medea is driven to her monstrous act by an uncontrollable frenzy. Many other incidental figures fill out the scene, including, as casual observers from above, Herakles, Athena, and the Dioskouroi; also the queen of Corinth, unable to help her daughter; and the customary nurse and paidagogos. Most interesting is an elderly barbarian king at the far right, inscribed "ghost of Aeetes." Medea's father, long dead, returns in spirit to remind his daughter of the betrayal of her hearth and home that has brought her ultimately to this sorry state.

The vase is a masterpiece of Late Apulian dramatic art. If it suffers from comparison with the Lucanian krater, that may be in part because the latter corresponds more closely to our modern ideas of narrative, in which a single dramatic moment, rendered in all its complexity and power, is the usual goal. The Lucanian krater also reminds us to what good effect the spatial relations of the picture panel could be put, by having the chariot carried aloft and dwarfing those left on the ground. The Apulian vase, by contrast, seems oppressively full, with Medea and her car squeezed into the lower register

Figure 129 Scenes from the Medea myth: death of the princess, Medea slays one child. Apulian volute-krater attributed to the Underworld Painter. Munich, Antikensammlungen 3296. Ca. 330–310.

under the massive weight of the architecture. Yet this type of scene was the standard for theatrical representations in Southern Italy, and the Lucanian vase rather the exception, another indication of how different the tastes and perceptions of the ancient viewer were from our own.

BIBLIOGRAPHY

The following references, which follow the organization of the text, are limited to works on Greek art and iconography. They do not include any sources that are principally about Greek literature or mythology, unless these are works that also include a substantial amount of iconographic material.

ABBREVIATIONS

Brommer, *Odysseus*: Brommer, F. (1983) *Odysseus*, Darmstadt: Wissenschaftliche Buchgesellschaft.

Johansen: Johansen, K. F. (1967) *The Iliad in Early Greek Art*, Copenhagen: Munksgaard.

Kossatz: Kossatz-Deissmann, A. (1978) *Dramen des Aischylos auf westgriechischen Vasen*, Mainz: Philipp von Zabern.

LIMC: *Lexicon Iconographicum Mythologiae Classicae* (1981–), Zurich and Stuttgart: Artemis-Verlag.

Prag: Prag, A. J. N. W. (1985) *The Oresteia*, Warminster: Aris & Philipps.

Schefold, *GHG*: Schefold, K. (1978) *Götter- und Heldensagen der Griechen in der spätarchaischen Kunst*, Munich: Hirmer. An English translation appeared while this book was in press: *Gods and Heroes in Late Archaic Greek Art*, Cambridge University Press. Page references given here are to the German edition.

Schefold, *Urkönige*: Schefold, K. (1988) *Die Urkönige, Perseus, Bellerophon, Herakles und Theseus in der klassischen und hellenistischen Kunst*, Munich: Hirmer.

Schefold, *SATT*: Schefold, K. and Jung, F. (1989) *Die Sagen von den Argonauten, von Theben und Troia in der klassischen und hellenistischen Kunst*, Munich: Hirmer.

Séchan: Séchan, L. (1926) *Etudes sur la tragédie grecque dans ses rapports avec la céramique*, Paris: Librairie ancienne Honoré Champion.

Touchefeu: Touchefeu-Meynier, O. (1968) *Thèmes odysséens dans l'art antique*, Paris: Editions E. de Bocard.

Trendall/Webster: Trendall, A. D. and Webster, T. B. L. (1971) *Illustrations of Greek Drama*, London: Phaidon.

GENERAL

The following are surveys and general handbooks of Greek art that include detailed treatments of the Archaic and Classical periods dealt with in this book, as well as handbooks of Greek vase-painting.

183

Boardman, J. (1975) *Athenian Black Figure Vases. A Handbook*, London: Thames & Hudson.

—— (1978) *Athenian Red Figure Vases. The Archaic Period*, London: Thames & Hudson.

—— (1989) *Athenian Red Figure Vases. The Classical Period*, London: Thames & Hudson.

Carpenter, T. H. (1990) *Art and Myth in Ancient Greece*, London: Thames & Hudson.

Hurwit, J. M. (1985) *The Art and Culture of Early Greece*, Ithaca, NY: Cornell University Press.

Pollitt, J. J. (1972) *Art and Experience in Classical Greece*, Cambridge: Cambridge University Press.

Robertson, M. (1975) *A History of Greek Art*, Cambridge: Cambridge University Press.

—— (1981) *A Shorter History of Greek Art*, Cambridge: Cambridge University Press.

—— (1992) *The Art of Vase-Painting in Classical Athens*, Cambridge: Cambridge University Press.

Simon, E., Hirmer, M., and Hirmer, A. (1981) *Die griechischen Vasen*, Munich: Hirmer.

Trendall, A. D. (1989) *The Red-Figure Vases of South Italy and Sicily*, London: Thames & Hudson.

NARRATIVE IN GREEK ART

The following list includes a few of the seminal works published between the late nineteenth century and the 1970s, as well as a reasonably comprehensive bibliography of studies published since 1978.

Boardman, J. (1989) "The Greek Art of Narrative," in Descœudres, J.-P. (ed.) *EUMOUSIA. Ceramic and Iconographic Studies in Honour of Alexander Cambitoglou*, Sydney: Mediterranean Archaeology, Supplement 1: 57–62.

—— (1991) "The Sixth-Century Potters and Painters of Athens and their Public," in Rasmussen, T. and Spivey, N. (eds.) *Looking at Greek Vases*, Cambridge: Cambridge University Press: 79–102.

Brilliant, R. (1984) *Visual Narratives*, Ithaca, NY: Cornell University Press.

Brommer, F. (1969) *Die Wahl des Augenblicks in der griechischen Kunst*, Munich: E. Heimerann.

Childs, W. A. P. (1991) "A New Representation of a City on an Attic Red-Figured Kylix," in *Greek Vases in the J. Paul Getty Museum* 5: 27–40.

Froning, H. (1988) "Anfänge der kontinuierenden Bilderzählung in der griechischen Kunst," *Jahrbuch des Deutschen Archäologischen Instituts* 103: 169–99.

—— (1992) "La forma rappresentative ciclica nell'arte classica," in Olmos, R. (ed.) *Coloquio sobre Teseo y la copa de Aison*, Madrid: Centro Estudios Historicos: 131–54.

Hanfmann, G. M. A. (1957) "Narration in Greek Art," *American Journal of Archaeology* 61: 71–78.

Himmelmann-Wildschütz, N. (1967) *Erzählung und Figur in der archaischen Kunst*, Wiesbaden: Franz Steiner.

Meyboom, P. G. P. (1978) "Some Observations on Narration in Greek Art," *Mededelingen van het Nederlands Instituut te Rome* 5: 55–82.

Raeck, W. (1984) "Zur Erzählweise archaischer und klassischer Mythenbilder," *Jahrbuch des Deutschen Archäologischen Instituts* 99: 1–25.

Robert, C. (1881) *Bild und Lied*, Berlin: Weidmann.

—— (1919) *Archäologische Hermeneutik*, Berlin: Weidmann.

Schefold, K. (1985) "Homer und der Erzählstil der archaischen Kunst," in *Eidolopoiia. Actes du colloque sur les problèmes de l'image dans le monde Méditerranéen classique*, Rome: Giorgio Brettschneider: 3–25. (In addition, all the other cited books by Schefold have discussions of narrative.)

Shapiro, H. A. (1990) "Old and New Heroes: Narrative, Composition, and Subject in Attic Black-Figure," *Classical Antiquity* 9: 114–48.

—— (1992) "Narrative Strategies in Euphronios," in Cygielman, M., Iozzo, M., Nicosia, F., and Zamarchi Grassi, P. (eds.) *Euphronios. Atti del Seminario Internazionale di Studi. Arezzo, 27–28 Maggio 1990*, Florence: Edizioni Il Ponte: 37–43.

Snodgrass, A. (1982) *Narration and Allusion in Archaic Greek Art*, London: Leopard's Head Press.

—— (1987) *An Archaeology of Greece*, Berkeley and Los Angeles: University of California Press: ch. 5, "The First Figure-scenes in Greek Art": 132–69.

Stewart, A. F. (1987) "Narrative, Genre, and Realism in the Work of the Amasis Painter," in *Papers on the Amasis Painter and his World*, Malibu: J. Paul Getty Museum: 29–44.

Stupperich, R. (1992) "Bildkombination und Ableserichtung auf klassischen Bildfriesschalen," in Brehm, O. and Klie, S. (eds.) *Mousikos Aner. Festschrift für Max Wegner zum 90. Geburtstag*, Bonn: Dr. Rudolf Habelt: 425–44.

Weitzmann, K. (1947) *Illustration on Roll and Codex*, Princeton: Princeton University Press: 12–22.

Wescoat, B. D. (1986) *Poets & Heroes: Scenes of the Trojan War*, exhibition catalog, Atlanta: Emory University Museum of Art and Archaeology: 6–10.

Wickhoff, F. (1900) *Roman Art*, trans. E. Strong, London: William Heinemann: 7–16.

EPIC

Iliad 1: Briseis

LIMC I, s.v. Agamemnon: 266.

LIMC III, s.v. Briseis: 157–61.

Johansen 153–60.

Kirk, G. S. (1985) *The Iliad: a Commentary*, vol. 1: books 1–4, Cambridge: Cambridge University Press.

Schefold, *SATT* 168–83.

Iliad 9: the embassy to Achilles

Döhle, H. (1967) "Die 'Achilleis' des Aischylos in ihrer Auswirkung auf die attische Vasenmalerei des 5. Jahrhunderts," *Klio* 49: 63–143.

Hellström, P. (1990) "Achilles in Retirement," *Medelhavsmuseet Bulletin* 25: 19–31.

LIMC I, s.v. Achilleus: 106–14.

Schefold, *SATT* 195–200.

Iliad 16: the death of Sarpedon

Bothmer, D. von (1981) "The Death of Sarpedon," in Hyatt, S. G. (ed.) *The Greek Vase*, Latham, NY: Hudson-Mohawk Association of Colleges and Universities: 63–80.

Clark, M. E. and Coulson, W. D. E. (1978) "Memnon and Sarpedon," *Museum Helveticum* 35: 65–73.
Robertson, M. (1988) "Sarpedon Brought Home," in Betts, J. H., Hooker, J. T., and Green, J. R. (eds.) *Studies in Honour of T. B. L. Webster*, vol. 2, Bristol: Bristol Classical Press: 109–20.

Iliad 22: the dragging of Hektor's body

LIMC I, s.v. Achilleus: 138–47.
Schefold, *GHG* 232–35.
Vermeule, E. (1965) "The Vengeance of Achilles," *Bulletin of the Museum of Fine Arts, Boston* 63: 34–52.

Iliad 23: the funeral games for Patroklos

Brownlee, A. B. (1988) "Sophilos and Early Attic Black-Figured Dinoi," in Christiansen, J. and Melander, T. (eds.) *Ancient Greek and Related Pottery*, Copenhagen: Nationalmuseet, Ny Carlsberg Glyptotek, & Thorvaldsens Museum: 80–85.
LIMC I, s.v. Achilleus: 119–20.
Roller, L. E. (1981) "Funeral Games in Greek Art," *American Journal of Archaeology* 85: 107–19.

Iliad 24: Priam and Achilles (the ransom of Hektor)

Basista, W. (1979) "Hektors Lösung," *Boreas* 2: 5–36.
Danali-Giole, A. (1981) *Ta "lytra tou Ektoros" eis ten technen tou ektou kai pemptou aionos*, Athens: Sophia N. Saripolou.
Isler, H. P. (1986) "Un idria del Pittore di Londra E76 con il riscatto di Ettore," *Numismatica e Antichità Classica* 15: 95–123.
LIMC I, s.v. Achilleus: 147–61.
Schefold, *GHG* 235–38.
Schefold, *SATT* 232–37.
Touchefeu-Meynier, O. (1990) "L'humiliation d'Hector," *Métis* 5: 157–65.

Odyssey 6: Odysseus and Nausikaa

Brommer, *Odysseus* 95–97.
Hauser, F. (1905) "Nausikaa," *Jahreshefte des Oesterreichischen Archäologischen Instituts* 8: 18–41.
LIMC VI, s.v. Nausikaa: 712–14.
Shapiro, H. A. (forthcoming 1994) "Coming of Age in Phaeacia: the Meeting of Odysseus and Nausikaa," in Cohen, B. (ed.) *The Distaff Side. Representing the Female in Homer's Odyssey*, Oxford: Oxford University Press.
Touchefeu 203–8.

Odyssey 9: the blinding of Polyphemos and the escape from the cave

Bothmer, D. von (1981) "A New Kleitias Fragment from Egypt," *Antike Kunst* 24: 66–67.
Brommer, *Odysseus* 57–67.
Fellmann, B. (1972) *Die antiken Darstellungen des Polyphemabenteuers*, Munich: Wilhelm Fink.

LIMC VI, s.v. Kyklops, Kyklopes: 154–59; s.v. Odysseus: 954–60.
Touchefeu 9–79.

Odyssey 10: Circe

Brommer, *Odysseus* 70–80.
LIMC VI, s.v. Kirke: 48–59.
Schefold, *GHG* 266–68.
Touchefeu 81–131.

Odyssey 22: the slaying of the suitors

Brommer, *Odysseus* 104–8.
LIMC VI, s.v. Mnesteres II: 631–4.
Pasquier, A. (1992) "Le massacre des prétendants: une nouvelle image de la cérami-
que campanienne par le Peintre d'Ixion," *Revue du Louvre* 42 (December): 13–39.
Schefold, *SATT* 319–25.
Touchefeu 256–63.

Hesiod: the creation of Pandora

Bérard, C. (1974) *Anodoi*, Rome: Institut Suisse de Rome.
Leipen, N. (1971) *Athena Parthenos*, Toronto: Royal Ontario Museum.
LIMC I, s.v. Anesidora: 790–91.
Loeb, E. H. (1979) *Die Geburt der Götter in der griechischen Kunst der klassischen
Zeit*, Jerusalem: Shikmona Publishing Co.: 142-64.
Schefold, K. (1981) *Die Göttersage in der klassischen und hellenistischen Kunst*,
Munich: Hirmer: 72–75.

LYRIC

Stesichoros: Herakles and Geryon

Brize, P. (1980) *Die Geryoneis des Stesichoros und die frühe griechische Kunst*,
Würzburg: Triltsch.
Jourdain-Annequin, C. (1989) *Héraclès aux portes du Soir*, Paris: Les Belles Lettres.
LIMC IV, s.v. Geryoneus: 186–90.
LIMC V, s.v. Herakles: 73–80.
Page, D. L. (1973) "Stesichorus: the *Geryoneis*," *Journal of Hellenic Studies* 93:
138–54.
Robertson, M. (1969) "*Geryoneis*: Stesichoros and the Vase-Painters," *Classical
Quarterly* 19: 207–21.
Schefold, *GHG* 113–20.

Pindar, *Olympian* 1: the chariot race of Pelops and Oinomaos

Lacroix, L. (1976) "La légende de Pélops et son iconographie," *Bulletin de
Correspondence Hellénique* 100: 327–41.
Saflund, M. L. (1970) *The East Pediment of the Temple of Zeus at Olympia*,
Göteborg: Paul Aströms.
Séchan 447–66.

Pindar, *Pythian* 2: Ixion on the wheel

Chamay, J. (1984) "Le châtiment d'Ixion," *Antike Kunst* 27: 146–50.

LIMC V, s.v. Ixion: 857–62.

Schefold, K. (1981) *Die Göttersage in der klassischen und hellenistischen Kunst*, Munich: Hirmer: 153–57.

Simon, E. (1955) "Ixion und die Schlangen," *Jahreshefte des Oesterreichischen Archäologischen Instituts* 42: 5–26.

Pindar, *Nemean* 9: the Seven against Thebes

Alfieri, N. and Arias, P. E. (1958) *Spina*, Munich: Hirmer: 43–46.

Boardman, J. (1992) "The Seven Go to War," in Froning, H., Mielsch, H. and Hölscher, T. (eds.) *Kotinos. Festschrift für Erika Simon*, Mainz: Philipp von Zabern: 167–70.

LIMC I, s.v. Adrastos: 231–40; s.v. Amphiaraos: 691–713.

Schefold, *SATT* 77–84.

Tiverios, M. (1981) "Sieben gegen Theben," *Athenische Mitteilungen* 96: 145–61.

Pindar, *Pythian* 4: Jason and the Argonauts

LIMC V, s.v. Iason: 631–34

Meyer, H. (1980) *Medeia und die Peliaden*, Rome: Giorgio Brettschneider.

Schefold, *SATT* 30–33.

Vojatzi, M. (1982) *Frühe Argonautenbilder*, Würzburg: Konrad Triltsch-Verlag.

Pindar, *Nemean* 3: Chiron and Achilles

Krieger, X. (1975) *Der Kampf zwischen Peleus und Thetis in der griechischen Vasenmalerei*, Münster: Westfälische Wilhelms-Universität.

LIMC I, s.v. Achilleus: 40–55.

LIMC III, s.v. Cheiron: 237–48.

Schefold, *GHG* 189–94.

Williams, D. (1983) "Sophilos in the British Museum," *Greek Vases in the J. Paul Getty Museum* 1: 9–34.

Pindar, *Nemean* 1: the infant Herakles

Brendel, O. (1932) "Der schlangenwürgende Herakliskos," *Jahrbuch des Deutschen Archäologischen Instituts* 47: 191–238.

Brommer, F. (1984) *Herakles* II: *die unkanonischen Taten des Helden*, Darmstadt: Wissenschaftliche Buchgesellschaft: 1–4.

LIMC IV, s.v. Herakles: 827–32.

Schefold, *Urkönige* 129–32.

Woodford, S. (1983) "The Iconography of the Infant Herakles Strangling Snakes," in Lissarague, F. and Thelamon, F. (eds.) *Image et céramique grecque*, Rouen: Université de Rouen: 121–30.

Bacchylides 18: Theseus' youthful deeds

Brommer, F. (1982) *Theseus*, Darmstadt: Wissenschaftliche Buchgesellschaft: 3–34.

Neils, J. (1987) *The Youthful Deeds of Theseus*, Rome: Giorgio Brettschneider.

Schefold, *GHG* 161–68.

Schefold, *Urkönige* 243–51.

Taylor, M. W. (1991) *The Tyrant Slayers*, Salem, NH: Ayers: ch. 4: "The Tyrannicides and the Labors of Theseus in Vase Painting": 36–70.

Bacchylides 17: Theseus at the bottom of the sea

Brommer, F. (1982) *Theseus*, Darmstadt: Wissenschaftliche Buchgesellschaft: 77–83.

Francis, E. D. (1990) *Image and Idea in Fifth-Century Greece*, London: Routledge: 58–65.

Isler-Kerenyi, C. (1977) *Lieblinge der Meermädchen*, Zurich: Archäologisches Institut der Universität.

Jacobsthal, P. (1911), *Theseus auf dem Meeresgrunde* Leipzig: E. A. Seamann.

Shapiro, A. (1982) "Theseus, Athens, and Troizen," *Archäologischer Anzeiger*: 291–97.

DRAMA

Aeschylus, *Agamemnon*: the murder of Agamemnon

Davies, M. I. (1969) "Thoughts on the *Oresteia* before Aischylos," *Bulletin de Correspondence Hellénique* 93: 214–60.

LIMC I, s.v. Agamemnon: 271–72.

Prag 1–5.

Schefold, *SATT* 298–309.

Vermeule, E. (1966) "The Boston Oresteia Krater," *American Journal of Archaeology* 70: 1–22.

Aeschylus, *Libation Bearers*: Electra and Orestes at the tomb of Agamemnon

Kossatz 92–97.

LIMC I, s.v. Elektra I: 709–14.

Trendall/Webster 40–44.

Aeschylus, *Libation Bearers*: the death of Aegisthus

Davies, M. I. (1969) "Thoughts on the Oresteia before Aischylos," *Bulletin de Correspondence Hellénique* 93: 214–60.

Kossatz 97–102.

LIMC I, s.v. Aigisthos: 371–79.

LIMC VI, s.v. Klytaimestra: 72–81.

Prag 6–34; 106–7.

Vermeule, E. (1966) "The Boston Oresteia Krater," *American Journal of Archaeology* 70: 1–22.

Aeschylus, *Eumenides*: Orestes at Delphi

Kossatz 102–17.

Prag 48–52.

Schefold, *SATT* 310–15.

Séchan 93–101.

Trendall/Webster 45–49.

Sophocles, *Ajax*: the suicide of Ajax

Davies, M. I. (1973) "Ajax and Tekmessa," *Antike Kunst* 16: 60–70.
—— (1985) "Ajax at the Bourne of Life," in *Eidolopoiia. Actes du colloque sur les problèmes de l'image dans le monde Méditerranéen classique*. Rome: Giorgio Brettschneider: 83–117.
Hurwit, J. (1982) "Palm Trees and the Pathetic Fallacy in Archaic Greek Poetry and Art," *Classical Journal* 77: 193–99.
LIMC I, s.v. Aias: 324–32
Schefold, *GHG* 250–52.
Schefold, *SATT* 259–65.

Sophocles, *Trachiniai*: the death of Nessos

Brommer, F. (1984) *Herakles* II: *die unkanonischen Taten des Helden*, Darmstadt: Wissenschaftliche Buchgesellschaft: 48–53.
Fittschen, K. (1970) "Zur Herakles–Nessos Sage," *Gymnasium* 77: 161–71.
LIMC VI, s.v. Nessos: 838–47.
Schefold, *GHG* 146–50.

Euripides, *Trojan Women*: the fall of Troy

Boardman, J. (1976) "The Kleophrades Painter at Troy," *Antike Kunst* 19: 3–18.
LIMC II, s.v. Astyanax I: 929–37.
Schefold, *GHG* 254–60.
Schefold, *SATT* 280–96.
Wiencke, M. I. (1954) "An Epic Theme in Greek Art," *American Journal of Archaeology* 58: 286–306.
Williams, D. (1991) "Onesimos and the Getty Iliupersis," *Greek Vases in the J. Paul Getty Museum* 5: 41–64.

Euripides, *Iphigenia among the Taurians*: Orestes and Iphigenia

LIMC V, s.v. Iphigeneia: 713–19.
Séchan 379–88.
Trendall/Webster 91–94.

Euripides, *Bacchae*: the death of Pentheus

Burn, L. (1987) *The Meidias Painter*, Oxford: Oxford University Press: 76–78.
Euphronios der Maler (1991) exhibition catalog, Berlin: Antikenmuseum: 174–77 (M. Padgett).
Glimpses of Excellence (1984) exhibition catalog, Toronto: Royal Ontario Museum: 16 (J. R. Guy).
Schöne, A. (1990) "Die Hydria des Meidias-Malers im Kerameikos," *Athenische Mitteilungen* 105: 171–76.

Euripides, *Medea*: the killing of the children and the escape from Corinth

LIMC VI, s.v. Medeia: 386–98.
Schefold, *SATT* 42–47.
Séchan 396–422.
Simon, E. (1954) "Die Typen der Medeadarstellung," *Gymnasium* 61: 203–27.

Trendall/Webster 96–97.

Wealth of the Ancient World (1983) exhibition catalog, Fort Worth, Kimbell Art Museum: 76–79 (J. M. Cody).

TRANSLATIONS

Excerpts from Greek literature are quoted, with permission, from the following translations.

The Iliad of Homer (1951) trans. Richmond Lattimore, Chicago: University of Chicago Press.

The Odyssey of Homer (1968) trans. Richmond Lattimore, New York: Harper & Row.

Hesiod, the Works and Days, Theogony, Shield of Herakles (1959) trans. Richmond Lattimore, Ann Arbor: University of Michigan Press.

Pindar's Victory Songs (1980) trans. Frank J. Nisetich, Baltimore: Johns Hopkins University Press.

The Art of Bacchylides (1985) by Ann Pippin Burnett, Cambridge, MA: Harvard University Press.

The Complete Greek Tragedies (1953–59) ed. David Grene and Richmond Lattimore, Chicago: University of Chicago Press:

Richmond Lattimore, trans., *Agamemnon, Libation Bearers, Eumenides, Trojan Women.*

John Moore, trans., *Ajax.*

Michael Jameson, trans., *Trachiniai* (The Women of Trachis).

Witter Bynner, trans., *Iphigenia in Tauris.*

William Arrowsmith, trans., *The Bacchae.*

Rex Warner, trans., *Medea.*

INDEX

192